R.O.I. POWER

R.O.I. POWER

**THE Step-by-Step Guide to Maximizing
Private Practice and Small Business Profits**

by
Richard "The ROI Guy" Seppala

Table of Contents

Introduction
Pumping Up Your ROI Power

There is your business, and then there is *your* business.

What do I mean by that? If somebody asked you what your business was, you would most likely describe it in terms of what you do. You would say that you are a dentist, or a real estate agent, or that you sell widgets online. In other words, your answer would be about whatever service or product you provide that brings you income.

Actually the word "business" has nothing to do with your occupation. Its real meaning relates to "doing commercially viable and profitable work" (I know, I looked it up in Wikipedia!).

Business is not about the type of work that you do, but rather, it is about whether it is making money. I do not mean to downgrade or disparage whatever you do to earn money because it must be something that people want or need, or they would not be paying for it. You are obviously providing value with what you do.

What I am saying is that whatever your business is about, you almost certainly want it to make the most profits possible (without, of course, doing anything illegal or immoral and if you are doing anything like that, keep me out of it!). The fact is that most business and private practice owners do not take the time to learn how to make the most profits. They focus on their expertise, which is, of course, essential to their success, but never study the principles of how to realize the best Return on Investment, or ROI.

This is where I come in. After all, I'm "The ROI Guy" and I do not want to see you leave money on the table every day you are open for business. It is the reason I wrote this book. For over a decade, I have helped businesses, both large and small, optimize their ROI in every way possible. Heck, I have even done it with my wife's business (she is a dentist), which you will read about later. Since we are still married, I must have done something right.

Now, I want to do something for you, and since you have already shown that you have excellent taste by reading this book, I am sure that I can!

This book is meant to be a step-by-step, top-to-bottom guide to creating the most "ROI Power" in any small or medium-sized business, or private practice. It is written in plain, understandable language, not business gibberish, and lays out proven ROI tactics and secrets in such a way that you can begin putting creating your own ROI Power.

ROI Power. It enables you to:
• Grow your business faster.
• Serve your customers better.
• Create a more enjoyable lifestyle for yourself and your family.
• Offer your employees (if you have any) more security.
• Automate systems that continue to generate prosperity.

Who would not want all that? If you do, read on. ROI Power is not about sleazy sales gimmicks or tricking people into giving you money. It is not about grinding down on yourself and your staff until you are exhausted from trying to make as much cash as you can.

Rather, it is about giving your current customers and potential leads the opportunity to take full advantage of what you have to offer by making yourself and your offerings as visible and available as possible. It is about creating a superior customer experience so that people will want to buy from you again and again. Not only that, but they tell their friends and family to buy from you as well. ROI Power is also about communicating with people who are most likely to buy from you in the most powerful way. Most of all, it is about gaining a mindset that allows you to look at your business in an entirely new way, with an attitude that is ROI-centric.

By the way, the great thing about ROI Power is that it is a renewable energy source and once this book teaches you the principles of ROI, you will be able to continue to put them into action as long as your doors (or online shopping carts!) are open for business.

Read on and get charged up. You are about to discover the ABCs of ROI. You will also read some interesting case studies about how some of my clients put ROI principles into play and changed the way they did business forever. After you have finished reading these pages, maybe you will do the same.

To *YOUR* ROI Power!

Section One
Understanding ROI Power

To me, ROI Power is a science and it is helpful to know the theories that make it work.

That is why, in this first section, I will introduce you to a few broad principles that underpin ROI and measuring that ROI. I will also compare what happens when somebody puts those principles into action with somebody who does not!
.

Chapter 1
Would You Want Your Kid to Flunk?
Or, Why ROI Matters

Your son has had problems with his grades. You get him to buckle down and work harder on homework and studying. When the anxiously awaited report card day rolls around, he comes home and hands you the all-important document. You are shocked to discover that instead of grades, the report card is filled with empty boxes.

You are trying to lose weight. You have been exercising more and eating cheeseburgers less. After a few weeks, you step on the scale to see how much progress you have made and you are rewarded with a bunch of blinking zeroes on the electronic display.

You are trying to cut down your ever-increasing electric bill. Diligently you replace all your light bulbs with those new-fangled bulbs that use a lot less energy and burn forever. At the end of the month, you check the electric meter to see how much you saved and it is blank!

None of these scenarios are much fun. In all three instances, you wanted concrete measurements to see what was happening in a situation that was important to you and you ended up without that information. In all three cases, I would be willing to bet that you would take steps to make sure you did not run into these informational dead ends again.

You would call the high school and demand to know why the grades were not provided. You would throw out the scale and get one that worked. You would call the electric company and make them fix the meter. You would do all these things because you needed to know what was going on. Otherwise, you could not properly evaluate the situations. Now, here is what is surprising to me. As I said, in each of those personal situations, you would make sure you had the facts so you could see exactly what, if any, improvement had occurred.

When it comes to your *business*, though, you might never apply this simple principle to your marketing. In other words, you might spend a certain amount of money on campaigns for the specific purpose of improving revenues and then *never measure whether those campaigns really worked.*

ROI matters and if you are not looking at it, you are looking for trouble. This brings me to my first of many ROI Rules (every chapter has one!).

ROI Guy Rule
If you don't measure, you don't know. And if you don't know, you're no better than a blind man at a bingo game.

Money for Nothing?

In almost every aspect of a business, everything from employee productivity to appropriately pricing products or services, the owner should be watching to see what the ROI truly is. It makes sense, right?

Businesses are all about making money and the logical way to proceed is to monitor the profit picture as closely as possible. Since you did not establish a company to spend money on everything in sight (unless you were looking for some kind of weird tax break!), it is critical to have a lock on what the ROI is for all your investments in your own company.

Since few business owners actually do, that leaves them in the position of having to make vital business decisions without having all the information they need to make the *right* decisions. Obviously, this kind of faulty process can be a business-killer.

Nowhere is that more true than with marketing because it is one of the primary aspects of a business that does not get measured. The fact is, especially with small and medium-sized businesses, marketing costs are not put to the test in the same way as other business expenses are.

Everyone knows they have to market and so they do it. Few, however, actually measure how much money those campaigns are actually bringing in because they do not know how to measure that particular ROI.

Instead, they rely on anecdotal information. A neighbor says, "Hey, I got your coupon in the mail today." A caller tells you that they saw your discount offer in the newspaper ad. Somebody else posts on their Facebook page about how cool your company's website is. Frankly, that kind of random feedback throws your marketing judgment completely out of whack because you do not think of it as random. Instead, you end up thinking one incident reflects a bigger trend. One positive comment may cause you to be overly generous toward one marketing effort. A negative comment may cause you to cut down or completely suspend another one.

You make these decisions even though you do not know really how well either one is working!!!

In the first case, you may be throwing more money at campaign that might look nice but does not actually motivate anyone to buy from you. In the second case, you might be bailing on marketing that is more effective, but you will never know because you did not give it a chance to play out.

That is not how the big boys play. Do you think McDonalds is not checking out how their marketing is their driving sales? Or Coca Cola? Or Ford? Huge corporations like those cannot afford not to measure their marketing ROI. They have to see a return on their big investment. To be honest, *so do you.*

Marketing Can Be Hazardous to Your Financial Health

I do not know if you are aware of this fact, but marketing can actually drive customers away from your door. Yes, you could be paying big bucks to lose business, resulting in a negative ROI. Not really what you want to see!

For example, you might be a dentist and have a great idea to create a special discount offer. The problem is, the person you hired to design the flyer advertising your offer made you look kind of cheap and low-rent. Combined with the discount, it makes you appear kind of desperate.

Cheap...low-rent...desperate.... Those are not the words you want to hear people use to describe your practice, are they? While the flyer might bring in some new low-rent clients, is this really how you want to target your practice?

Perhaps you are a lawyer who puts up a special website attract people with big IRS tax problems. You hired your nephew, the copywriter, to write the website for you and it is filled with typos and misspellings. He even spells "IRS" as "ISR" in one place. Is anyone going to trust a tax lawyer who cannot spell "IRS?"

I admit that the last example might be a little silly but how many so-called professional sites have you been on where you have found misspellings galore? Or language written by someone for whom English is obviously not their native tongue.

Any kind of professional is hurt by a non-professional presentation. I am using very obvious examples here, but let me be clear; how you are marketing can come off as non-professional in a very subtle way. As the experts will tell you, sometimes merely using the wrong color in a campaign will turn people off.

If you are not measuring your marketing ROI, you might never know how much you are losing on your advertising investments.

The converse is true as well. As I said earlier, you also might not know if a marketing campaign is wildly successful and that could mean you unwittingly kill a goose that is laying some serious golden eggs.

Suppose you put a beautiful full page ad for your business in a local annual directory. It presents you and your services in the best possible way. Buying the space was kind of expensive and after a year when it is time to decide whether to continue the ad or not, you hesitate.

You review the numbers and to see what else you might be able to do with the money instead of renewing the ad. Maybe you could do three ads for the price of that one in other places. Or perhaps you want to refocus your campaigns and do strictly online advertising.

After thinking it over, you pull the plug. When you pulled it, you thought you were making a decision based on the numbers. The only problem is that you did not actually have the numbers. The expensive ad listed your standard office phone number as your contact number, which meant you had no idea how much new business came to you because of the ad. They could have been calling you because of the Yellow Pages, your website, or the ad.

If you had been tracking the ROI of that directory ad with a special telephone tracking number, you might have been surprised to find out the ad more than paid for itself. As a matter of fact, it might have gained you several new loyal customers, who would provide ongoing revenue for years to come. Instead, you pulled the ad because it incurred some short term pain in your budget. However, in another 12 months, you could discover that you have even less to spend on marketing because your revenues dipped year-to-year for some unknown reason.

Mysteries Are For TV Shows

When you watch CSI or NCIS or any of the other multitude of crime dramas on network television, you get to see the star solve a murder that has already happened (and the star usually solves it in an hour or less—pretty impressive!). When it comes to ROI, however, once the crime has been committed, it is usually too late to solve it. For example, let us go back to marketing. You cannot track the ROI after the fact because that ship has already sailed. You already spent the money on the campaigns and people already responded (or did not respond). You could go back and ask the customers you picked up during the past year which marketing motivated them to come to you, but the odds are overwhelming that they either will not remember or they will misremember. Your business is obviously a lot more important to you than it is to them and, frankly, they are not going to devote a valuable chunk of their memories to the story of how you two crazy kids got together.

Measuring ROI is your responsibility as a business owner and it is an important one. You want to know what is making you money and what is costing you money. It is the only way to build a business because you are able to put more resources into what works, and take away those that do not. It is like the old joke about how to carve an elephant sculpture out of a giant piece of rock—you cut away everything that does not look like an elephant.

Without having solid ROI measurements, you are in a constant state of confusion about why you are either profitable or in the red. That kind of mystery you do not need in your life because, trust me, unlike the TV detectives, you are not going to solve it in an hour, with or without commercials.

ROI Power—Going Beyond the Bucks

Incidentally, when it comes to your business, you should not measure your ROI Power merely in terms of dollars and cents.

I believe there are four main "Power Pillars" of business ROI that need to be measured on an ongoing basis. These are the four most important things I believe every business owner invests in on a daily basis and deserves a return on, if everything is handled properly. You do not want to see any of these Power Pillars go to waste.

Let's quickly look at each one of them:

ROI Power Pillar #1: Money

This is the pillar that I have been discussing throughout this chapter, but I want to make one more point. Some people think that the more money they spend, the more they will get back, the old "it takes money to make money" school of thought. There is no question having a lot of money available opens up a lot of options but it is also true that you do not necessarily solve a problem by throwing money at it. When you measure your ROI, you know where to put money to make you more money.

ROI Power Pillar #2: Time

Every small business owner finds his biggest nemesis is often the clock. There are only so many hours in the day and only so many tasks that you can get done at an optimal level. This means your time can be as precious an investment as money when it comes to your ROI and you do not want to waste it on projects that do not pay off.

That is why it is often more cost-effective to hire people to do more of the day-to-day drudgery or, at the very least, automate the tasks as much as possible. For example, I provide many automated marketing systems that track ROI and also trigger follow-up marketing to warm leads. These are the kinds of systems that help a business owner make maximum use of his or her time.

ROI Power Pillar #3: Brand

This one might sound strange to the average business owner. You might ask yourself, "How do I invest in my brand? If you run your business in a way that establishes you as a trustworthy and reliable professional, then you are investing all those attributes in your brand.

You will read more about this in a later chapter. Your brand is easily your most crucial intangible asset. It is something that you have worked hard to build up in order to have a good word-of-mouth reputation that attracts new business. When you build a strong brand, you can receive a very strong return on it because, once established, it continues to work for you without you lifting a finger.

ROI Power Pillar #4: Employees

Your employees can be "The Perfect Storm" when it comes to creating a disastrous ROI because you put your time, money *and* image, (all three of the previous pillars), into the people you hire to work at your business. Think about everything you invest in them: you have to spend time training them, you have to pay them, and you have to make them aware of the objectives of your business. It is a huge investment.

This is a critical one, especially when it comes to staff that regularly interacts with potential and existing customers. You absolutely need a high ROI from those particular employees. If they are not treating your customers right, or if they have no training in to how sell your services in the most pro-active way, then they are actively damaging your business daily. This is a situation that needs a remedy.

When you measure the four Power Pillars of your ROI, you understand where your business is working and why. Measuring your ROI makes a huge difference to your bottom line and it is why I have based my career on helping businesses both measure and improve theirs.

You can be sure that your business is on the path to success when your ROI Power is fully charged.

Chapter 2
The KPI Countdown

The Big 5 You Need to Measure Maximum ROI Power

It is time for a new acronym. Or perhaps, "KP"I is not a new acronym for you because Key Performance Indicators have become a hot commodity over the past few years. Thanks to evolving technological breakthroughs, corporations all over the world are more easily able to monitor their revenues, expenses, sales and operational data and use that to create BI (Business Intelligence) that allows them to more effectively run their companies so that profits are maximized. All of that is a very long-winded way of saying that, because these guys know what is going on, they save money.

There are literally hundreds (if not thousands) of different KPI's that companies are measuring. Sometimes, the KPI is designed to measure how much progress is being made toward a strategic goal. At other times, it is designed to measure the ongoing level of success of an operational objective (zero manufacturing defects, high customer satisfaction, and so forth). Frequently, it is about dollars and cents, for example when it measures how much a certain business activity is costing versus how much revenue it is bringing in (in other words, back to our favorite acronym, ROI!).

The point is, selecting the right KPIs to make the right measurements can be a very complicated process due to the often-bewildering array of choices you have to pick from. When you want to measure how long a sofa is, you only need a tape measure. However, it is much different when you want to measure the efficiency of your manufacturing facility since you have to make sure you are looking at the right variables.

Okay, let us hit the brakes. If your brain is starting to shut down because you do not have your own manufacturing facility and you are not really thinking about getting one in the near future—do not worry—this is about to become very relevant to your business or practice.

This is why; the technology that is delivering the data that helps big companies make more money can also help you, no matter what size your business is. This is because that technology is now very accessible, affordable and easy to use. That brings us to this chapter's "ROI Rule":

ROI Guy Rule
Make sure you're measuring the right thing to determine ROI. To know how big a couch is, you don't just measure the cushion!

In this chapter, we are going to countdown the "Big 5" of KPIs that you should use to measure your marketing success in your small or medium-sized business or practice. As I walk you through these, I will also talk about why these specific KPIs are important and what they reflect about your marketing effectiveness.

KPI #5: Website Traffic, Activity and Conversion

Let us face it, the *Yellow Pages* are almost dead and buried. When it comes to finding you and finding out *about* you, your potential customers, clients or patients are almost certainly going to head over to your website on their laptop, tablet or Smartphone in order to evaluate whether or not your business meets their needs.

Most people check out products and providers online before they actually buy from them. The Internet makes it easy to get a sense of who you are and what your business is about. Over half of all consumers use it in order to make their purchasing decisions.

That means your website is carrying a lot of responsibility for your future success, especially if your marketing is aimed at driving traffic toward your website. Your site needs to do a lot of "heavy lifting" when a visitor first loads up your home page, therefore, you want to have the proper tools in place to engage them, and to motivate them to leave contact information in order for you to convert them to a sale.

Since these tools are so important, you want to be able to ascertain whether they are actually working. There are *several* important KPI measurements in this category that you should automatically monitor on an ongoing basis. These measurements help you to know for a fact that your website is doing all it can do to motivate a lead to buy from you (or, at the very least, opt in to your marketing list).

The first and most basic KPI is measuring the number of *unique* visitors every month to your site (you can also measure this number every week, every day, or even every hour, depending on how sophisticated your tracking system is). Note that I said "unique" visitors; you do not want to be counting the same people more than once. Your uncle may be very proud of you and checks out your site eighty times a day, but that does not mean you should include all those repeated visits in your total!

Another important KPI under this heading is how much time a visitor is spending on your site. This is a critical number because most people size up a website in a few seconds and either leave it or stay to poke around a little more. If you notice that visitors are not hanging around to find out more about your operation or your products and services, your home page has a big problem because it is not converting at a very basic level.

You also want to measure your opt-in rate, if you have any kind of offer on your site that requires the visitor to leave a name and email address. By stacking up the number of unique visitors against the number of opt-ins you are getting, you can get a good idea how strong your offer is. You will want to play with the offer to see what gets you the best opt-in rate.

Finally, how many visitors are actually either placing an order online or calling your office to place an order or book an appointment? It is easy to track the former, but the only way to track the latter is to use a unique phone tracking number on your website. This will enable you to distinguish which calls are being motivated by your website content. Comparing the raw number of unique visitors verses orders/calls will give you your actual conversion rates. In most cases, this rate is well below 10%, so do not despair if you are in single digits. Always be on the lookout for different content or marketing messages that will improve your conversion rates.

KPI #4: Lead Generation

It is essential that you know how many leads your various marketing campaigns generate and how well they enter your sales conversion process. After all, you are spending money, time and effort on marketing for the purpose of getting new people interested in your business!

This is where a marketing tracking system is really indispensable. When you put a unique phone number on every campaign and you have the systems in place to track those calls at your office or store, you will automatically know how many leads are being generated by each campaign. The value of that is hard to deny. When you know which campaigns are generating the most leads, you know which are the most effective in reaching your target market.

KPI #3: Database DNA

This is not, strictly speaking, a KPI of your marketing, but it is a vitally important measurement that is awesome to have in place when you are ready to move forward with a marketing campaign.

It is a well-known business truism that, generally speaking, 20% of your customer base generates 80% of your revenues; in other words, your best customers are the lifeblood of your business.

You want more like those 20%, right? Database DNA allows you to find more of them because your "best customer" pool shares various attributes. Once you identify those attributes, you can go ahead and specifically target similar leads with, for instance, a direct mail campaign, and your response rate will skyrocket. That is because these are the kind of people who are *most likely* to buy from you and will be the most open to your marketing messages. *These* are the kind of leads you want to market to.

KPI #2: Your Marketing Funnel Visualization

In the next chapter, I am going to discuss sales and marketing funnels in depth. For now, you need to know that the top of the funnel is where you attract leads into your marketing system, the middle is where you identify those leads (i.e., get them to opt-in and leave their contact information) and the bottom of the funnel is where they actually buy from you.

At every level of the funnel, you want to be able to review the numbers of how well you are engaging your leads. If there is a weak rate of engagement at any of the funnel's stages, then as the saying goes, "a chain is only as strong as its weakest link." When you can put the finger on where your weak link is, you are able to adjust the message or content at that level in order to ensure that you are moving along enough of the initial group of leads to where you want them to go.

Obviously, you are always going to lose some leads along the way, no matter what you do, but you can definitely improve your retention and conversion rates by recalculating your marketing formulas a little. The only way to see how that recalculating is actually *affecting* your engagement rates though is by measuring how many leads are progressing through the funnel every step of the way.

To do this effectively, you should have an all-in-one, top-to-bottom, marketing tracking system in place. For example, I constructed my ROI Matrix to follow each generated lead as they progress through each part of the marketing process until they "buy or die." My clients are able to access lead activity through an online dashboard that shows the latest data in real time. This kind of at-a-glance approach allows a business owner to see instantly how well a marketing funnel is working and where there might be problems that need to be addressed.

KPI #1: Marketing ROI

Marketing ROI is where the rubber hits the road. It is the ultimate marketing measurement because it shows you exactly how much money you are making from each specific marketing campaign versus the campaign's expense. In other words, it answers the all-important question, are you profiting from a marketing campaign, or is it actually working at a *loss?*

Business is all about dollars and cents; that is why we call it the bottom line, right? Yet, many companies and practices simply market without making their marketing accountable and that is simply because they do not know how.

This is where a marketing tracking system (like my ROI Matrix, yes, this is another plug!) can make a huge difference. You might say, "Well, I already know how many leads my campaigns are generating and I do not need to know the exact numbers." I beg to differ. A campaign might attract a thousand leads but they either do not generate sales, or only produce a few dollars here and there. On the other hand, a campaign may attract only three or four leads but, if you were marketing a fairly high-end product or service, that campaign may end up paying for itself three or four times over; in other words, it generated a huge profit.

That is why measuring the final dollar amount resulting from a marketing campaign is the absolute test of its effectiveness. All the other KPIs I have discussed in this chapter are equally important, but the beauty of a fully integrated marketing tracking system is that it will automatically make most of those measurements as well as the overall campaign ROI.

Marketing should not be guesswork. In this day and age, there is no reason for that approach. The more relevant numbers you have at your fingertips about your marketing campaigns, the more profitable they will be and the more you will save by eliminating campaigns that do not make money.

Make sure you are in a position to get accurate readings on the KPIs I have discussed in this chapter. These kinds of meaningful measurements make marketing less of a crapshoot and more of a science and also allow you to make the *right* changes when your campaigns and funnels are functioning, as they should.

Chapter 3
Top-to-Bottom Profit

The Facts Behind Sales Funnels

Let us talk about funnels. You know what a funnel looks like, right? If not, this should refresh your memory:

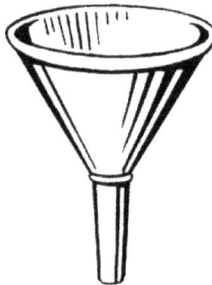

Unless you order out every night, you obviously know that funnels are often used in the kitchen. Of course they have other uses as well, such as putting motor oil in your car. More importantly, as it pertains to in this chapter, they are used to make money for businesses. In this instance, I am not talking about an actual *physical* funnel such as the one pictured above but rather I am talking about funnel *systems*.

Funnel systems are designed to attract a wide range of people with a casual interest in your business, product or service and take those people through a process that will turn a certain percentage of them into either quality ongoing leads or paying customers.

Why is it called a *funnel* system? Like a physical funnel that narrows as it grows closer to the bottom, in the funnel system, the number of people who stay engaged in the process invariably shrink, as the system takes them closer and closer to a specific end goal. You end up narrowing your initial group down to smaller, but valuable, leads or customers.

In this chapter I am going to explore with you the two main types of funnel systems: sales and marketing funnels. Even though they are both important for entirely different reasons and they have entirely different goals, they are extremely vital to any business. Which brings us to a new "ROI Rule":

ROI Guy Rule
Funnel your prospects down to your most likely buyers and build customers for life!

Let us look at how that works, starting with the sales funnel.

The Sizzle of the Sales Funnel

A sales funnel, also known as a sales tunnel, is designed to directly convert a lead to a sale. Success is measured by how many initial leads actually end up making a purchase.

A sales funnel is actually a fairly straightforward process. For example, you might have 500 people visit your website and that would be the top of your funnel. Generally speaking, this initial group will be composed of a mix of qualified leads that are ready to buy, unqualified leads that are still on the fence, and unqualified but interested parties.

While they are on your home page, 50 of those 500 might click on a link for more information about a specific product or service and that would be the middle of the funnel. Finally, 5 of those 50 people might actually go through with the checkout process and buy from you and that would be the bottom of your funnel. Since 5 out of your initial 500 leads bought, that gives your sales funnel a 1% conversion rate.

Similarly, another sales funnel might involve attracting people to watch your free webinar or YouTube video online. The webinar/video will contain information that will offer a solution to a common problem for those watching it and relates it right back to whatever you are selling. It ends with a pitch for your product as well as an embedded link to your sales page. Some viewers will be motivated enough to click on the link and go to the sales page; a small percentage of those people will be motivated to continue on to the order page, and a smaller percentage of those will actually pull the trigger and put in their credit card numbers.

In every sales funnel, you are creating a direct path that travels from initial contact—to product information—to the checkout cart. On that path, you are starting with unaware buyers, then separating out the interested buyers and winnowing them down until you finally arrive with the folks who are actually going to make a purchase.

The sales funnel is a very popular tool with businesses. It is incredibly easy to determine your ROI on a sales funnel by taking a quick look at your conversion rate. Since the end game is always the generating of immediate revenues, it also gives you immediate gratification (as well as immediate bucks!). That always feels good.

However, just as in life, it is not always about living in the moment, sometimes you need to build toward a bigger, better future and that is why marketing funnels are much more critical to ongoing profits than sales funnels.

The Magic of the Marketing Funnel

Yes, sales funnels are awesome if you want to try and sell as much of a product or service at once as possible. For example, if you are hawking a lone book or informational DVD, without being concerned about building long-term growth for your business, a sales funnel is the best solution. It is ideal for a one-shot product.

However, when it comes to businesses like a medical or dental practice, law firm, or financial services company, a marketing funnel creates the best conditions for sustained success. With a marketing funnel, you are working toward attracting and engaging lifetime clients and customers who will continue to buy from you over the years, the lifeblood of any business. The value of those leads over the long haul is astronomic.

Go ahead and take a look at your business and try to ballpark the amount of money you stand to make from someone who repeatedly patronizes your business over twenty years or more. The number should either make you very, very happy or motivate you to consider raising your rates!

There are generally three stages to a marketing funnel:

Stage 1 (the top): Traffic Generation
You have to interest potential leads in what you are selling. Frequently, this is done by an "irresistible offer" of either a free special report or DVD, or a discount on something you are selling. This initial engagement should be as powerful as possible, in order to gather the largest group possible at the top of your funnel.

Stage 2 (the middle): Lead Identification
The irresistible offer of Stage 1 should be designed to entice the interested lead to leave his or her contact information through an "opt-in" form. If you are working with a sophisticated marketing team such as mine, then

obtaining that contact information will enable you, in many cases, to "prequalify" the lead in terms of their buying power (credit, past buying history, etc.).

Stage 3 (the bottom): Follow-Up Marketing

With the qualified lead loaded into your CRM (Customer Relationship Management) software, you are now able to continue to contact him or her, either through emails, "snail mail, and "phone calls, or special marketing" touches." These touches are often most effective when they are mostly educational. They should provide credible information about the seriousness of a specific problem and how powerful your marketing solution is.

In the past, entrepreneurs and small businesses have been wary of marketing funnels. There was no real "hard sell" in most of these systems and it was almost impossible to analyze their real ROI, since they were aimed at multiple sales down the line and not a quick buck at the moment.

Years ago, follow-up marketing was also time-consuming and difficult; most companies did not have the manpower and resources to pull it off consistently and effectively.

Today's technology has changed all those negatives into one giant *positive*.

The Hi Tech Miracle

Marketing funnels can effectively address an increasingly complex marketing environment better than any other system because we are now able to do incredible things with them. (There is an additional big reason that you will read about near the end of this chapter).

First of all, with the advanced marketing tracking technology available today, you can easily measure the ROI of a marketing funnel and see how much money a well-crafted one can bring in to your business.

Secondly, CRM software makes it incredibly easy to gather lead contact information and turn it to do the all-important follow-up marketing that needs to take place. Without that follow-up, any marketing funnel is truly incomplete.

Why is that follow-up so important? Simple, because *that is where most sales are made.*

Check out these statistics from the National Sales Association:

1st Contact:	2 percent of sales are made
2nd Contact:	3 percent of sales are made
3rd Contact:	5 percent of sales are made
4th Contact:	10 percent of sales are made
5th-12 Contact:	**80 percent of sales are made**

Does that last statistic blow your mind? Yes, you read it right—over *80 percent of sales are made after you have contacted a lead five or more times.* This should help you understand why a marketing funnel can be much more powerful than a sales funnel. A marketing funnel sets you up for the second, third, fourth, and fifth contact (or, as I like to call it, "touch") which puts the odds more in your favor toward an eventual sales conversion.

As I have indicated earlier, the marketing funnel was an unwieldy system to pull off and was not viewed as cost effective. What has changed is the automation that can now be applied to these funnel systems. With the right system, you can keep track of leads from the moment they enter your funnel (sales *or* marketing) to their final "buy or die" decision.

More importantly, since you have this information on all the leads in your funnel, you can easily determine the actual ROI Power of a marketing funnel, in other words, you can stack up the expense of specific marketing versus the revenues it generates, to see if a campaign or funnel is profitable or not.

Before we were able to build these hi-tech systems, the process of determining the "True ROI" of a marketing campaign was almost impossible, if you wanted to end up with an accurate result. The process required going through all your records for months, or even years, and adding up the right numbers. In spite of all that work, you were likely to miss something important. Now, you do not have to miss a thing.

Why Funnels Are Important Now

Way, way back in the 20th Century, pretty much all you needed to market was a strong "static message" that you could send out to as many people as possible. What do I mean by static message? Turn on your TV and wait for a commercial (it will not take long!) and you will see one.

Static messages are usually delivered through what is called "old media". TV commercials are a prime example of them, as are radio commercials, billboards and magazine/newspaper ads. The advertisers are trying to tell you, as effectively as possible, why you should buy their product or why their company is better than then their competitor's. The static message is self-contained and the audience is a passive participant. You either listen to the message or you do not and then it is gone.

By contrast, marketing and sales funnels are meant to be *interactive,* not static. They encourage the lead to actually take a next step at that moment and the next step is specifically crafted to encourage the lead to take yet another step, until hopefully, the sale or opt-in is a done deal. There are two primary reasons the successful marketer has evolved past the static message to the interactive.

Reason number one: Technology has enabled the more interactive experience to be possible to such an extent that it has reached back into the old media. In the last couple of years, you have probably seen QR codes plastered all over all sorts of conventional advertising. QR codes are the boxed bar code-like configurations that are readable by Smartphones with the proper application installed. When QRs are read, the device doing the reading immediately links to the website of the marketer, usually a landing page featuring the specific product or service being advertised.

Reason number two: *Most of us have become immune to static messages!* We have grown up being constantly bombarded by them and we dismiss 99.9% of them as marketing ads that we do not need to pay any attention to. Occasionally, we might see an ad for a new movie we are interested in, or a commercial that makes us laugh, but when is the last time you paid attention to a commercial for laundry detergent or for a car you are never going to consider buying?

Instead, what is more important than ever is *lead engagement.* This process is a well-designed funnel that begins with an irresistible offer and continues by putting forward a powerful solution to a common problem that will engage leads and keep them moving through your sales or marketing process, resulting in big business for your company.

Marketing and sales funnels are perfect for our wired generation. Most of us are carrying around Smartphones and tablets 24/7 that enable continued exposure to our funnels. Social media is also an amazing base to begin the top of your funnel.

This interactive element will increase in importance as we continue to live more of our lives in the virtual realm. You will want to make sure you funnel the new technology to your advantage in all your marketing efforts. It does not pay to remain static anymore!

Chapter 4
ROI vs. 'R' You Crazy?

A Tale of Two Professionals

In this chapter, we are going to have a little fun (sorry it took this long). However, before I go any further, I want to explain something. My title as "The ROI Guy" legally obligates me to be as pro-ROI as possible.

Federal law dictates that, in order for me to hang onto that moniker, I must take every possible opportunity to advocate that businesses, professionals and entrepreneurs measure their Return On Investment to the maximum extent possible. Talk about big government, right? Okay, I am kidding (see, we are already having fun!). Congress really has not passed any legislation regarding the enforcement of my "ROI Guy" title. Even I know I am not that important and even if I was, those jokers cannot even pass a budget, let alone do anything about me!

Enough political talk, let us get back to ROI Power since ROI Power is important to me. It was important to me when I worked at a large national corporation and it is still important now that my mission is to help all different size businesses market smarter, sell more, and boost their bottom lines. By the way, ROI Power should be important to you as well.

How important is creating and measuring your ROI Power? Let me show you two examples of two very different marketers with two very different approaches to their businesses.

I have named these guys Dan the Dentist and Larry the Lawyer. They do not exist in real life, so there is no need to try and figure out who I am really talking about. However, what happens to them as a result of their marketing mechanics is very realistic, trust me.

The Dentist Who Wouldn't Drill Deep

I am going to begin with the story of Dan the Dentist. In order to achieve his ambition of being a great dentist, Dan worked hard when he went to college and dental school. He was able to start his own practice after graduation and his patients were ecstatic about his dedication to providing them with the best possible care. The only problem was that he did not have enough of them.

Running a practice is expensive. Dan had to pay for his equipment, a receptionist, a hygienist, and rent on his office space. Plus, he tended to give his friends big discounts. As for his relatives, he did not even charge them for his services. There were occasional months when he was not making a profit. He kept telling himself his practice would grow and he acted more confident than he really was.

One year, he went to a dentists' conference in Orlando, Florida. When he was attending a seminar, he shared his problem with another dentist, Darla (yes, all dentists in this story have first names that begin with "D"). Darla listened carefully and then asked, "How's your marketing?"

Dan shrugged. He explained that he did not really like marketing because it made him feel kind of sleazy. He was not a salesperson; he was a dentist and a pretty good one. He had hired someone to design a very professional website for his practice, he sent reminder postcards to his patients, and he had his listing in the Yellow Pages in bold print, all the normal stuff. For him, hardcore marketing brought thoughts of diet pills and energy drinks, not professional services.

Darla shook her head. "Don't you know there are more dentists than ever before? Competition is getting more and more brutal and you have to sell yourself in order to separate your practice from the others? We have to market ourselves just like any other business in order to survive. I do a bunch of campaigns every year, I measure the ROI of every one of them and I know what works and what doesn't. That saves my life, trust me."

Dan looked at her quizzically. "R-O-what?"

Darla explained all about "Return On Investment" and why he had to make sure his marketing was *making* him money, not *losing* him money. She talked about direct mail, referral programs, Google ads, website SEO, and social media marketing. Darla went on to explain why he had to "drill deep" into his tracking data to evaluate which was the most profitable. Even if Dan did not have the time or motivation to do it all, Darla assured him that there were a lot of good marketing consultants who could do it for him.

As she thoughtfully explained all his options, Dan stared at her and thought to himself...

"I wonder if she'll go out with me?"

"Are you listening to me?" she finally asked.

"Yeah, .but I'm not a businessman. I'm a dentist. I just want to be a dentist, and if I'm good at that, everything else should work out."

"Dan," she replied, "You're ignoring a very big fact—you're a dentist AND a businessman. You're already running a business, so don't you think you should find out more about how to do that? Would you get behind the wheel of a car without learning how to drive first? No! You have to learn marketing to survive. Where are you going to get new patients?"

"They'll hear about me from my patients and they'll give us a call," he said with a defiant nod, adding, "So what are you doing for dinner?"

Rolling her eyes, she replied, "Something else," and moved on.

When Dan got home, he thought about what Darla said. Perhaps, he thought, I should do some marketing. Then next year, I can tell Darla all about how I turned it all around and she will agree to have dinner with me."

Dan went a little crazy. He spent more than he should have on a whole bunch of campaigns. He did a direct mail campaign, he put a coupon in the Val-U-Pak for a complimentary bottle of water for new patients and he hired his cousin Eddie to do a lot of online ads. Eddie was good for that because he was smart about computers. He decided he did not have to worry about measuring any "RO's something"—whatever that last letter was, that Darla had been talking about. That would make marketing more expensive. He decided it would be better to spend all the money on more marketing, and then he could measure his results by the number of new patients that came in.

At first, things seemed to be going the way he wanted them to. Three new patients called to book appointments. When they came into the office, he asked them what made them call his practice. They could not remember. Two out of the three only wanted a quick exam to make sure nothing was wrong. Then nothing more happened.

Dan gave it some more thought. If he could figure out what campaign had brought in the three patients, he could repeat it. Obviously it had not been the coupon because nobody had asked for the bottle of water. Cousin Eddie said he thought there was a way to track the online ads, but he was not sure.

Dan decided it must have been the direct mail campaign. That was a killer. He had mailed giant postcards with a cartoon tooth on the front yelling, "Hey! You might have a cavity! Come see Dan the Dentist before it gets infected!"

He sent out a lot more of those postcards. But nothing happened. What Dan did not know was that one of Eddie's Google Ad Words campaigns, which were incredibly cheap, had actually pulled in those three prospects but Dan never told Eddie to keep it going, so Eddie pulled the plug. Instead, Dan spent a lot more on the direct mail than he should have.

Dan was out of marketing money. To make matters worse, two of his biggest-spending patients were moving out of the area. He was actually *losing* customers.

When Darla saw Dan the following year at the conference, she discovered that he had been forced to close his own practice and go work for another dental practice near his. She felt sorry for him, and no, she did not go out to dinner with him.

The Lawyer Who Knew the Laws of Marketing

Larry was an attorney who specialized in helping people and businesses with their IRS tax troubles. He was doing okay, but he knew that he had to continually attract new clients for his particular practice. They had to know he was there to help.

Larry began to study marketing approaches and attending seminars. One day he heard about this great marketing expert, who was called the ROI Guy or something like that, who could help him put in place automatic systems that would make it easy for Larry and his staff to market consistently and follow-up with leads. These systems would also automatically measure the ROI of each specific marketing campaign.

By monitoring his marketing ROI, Larry would be able to determine which marketing message was most effective, and also which advertising venue generated the most new leads for his practice. This required Larry to use unique tracking phone numbers on each of his campaigns. By having a different phone number on each marketing placement, he would know instantly which campaign had generated a lead.

Through a process of trial-and-error with some limited campaigns, Larry was able to ascertain that the most powerful way to interest new clients was to educate potential clients about what he did and make them feel comfortable about working with a lawyer on their tax issues. He posted free YouTube videos featuring himself discussing common tax issues and the solutions to those issues.

He then created specific landing pages for these tax issues and embedded a link to the landing pages at the end of the videos. He also posted the videos on his Facebook page and used Facebook advertising to target people who could afford his services.

By measuring his ROI on each of these placements, he was able to focus his marketing efforts on the least expensive and most profitable campaigns. He eliminated marketing expenses that did not generate viable leads. His automated follow-up marketing enabled him to do conversions down the road with leads who did not buy right away. He even utilized valuable free marketing tools such as Google maps to promote his business. All in all, he was able to attract a steady stream of new clients that helped him build his practice.

His law firm grew. Through online advertising, he was able to obtain clients out of his area, all across the country, as a matter of fact. He hired other lawyers who did the bulk of his work for him, giving him more time to enjoy his life and the extra money his marketing machinery had provided for him.

He also attended marketing seminars in different cities in order to remain current on the latest marketing techniques. At one of these seminars, which happened to be in Orlando, Florida, he met a nice dentist named Darla. They enjoyed a wonderful dinner together and eventually got married and had three beautiful children. Talk about ROI Power!

To ROI or Not to ROI

I will admit our Tale of Two Marketers offers two extremes: one professional who did everything wrong and another who did everything *right*. Even though I told you those people do not really exist, I actually know a guy like Larry the Lawyer who does have a legal firm specializing in tax cases and does all the marketing stuff I said that Larry did. He has enjoyed the level of success that "Larry" did because he paid attention to that marketing data. However, he did not marry a nice dentist named Darla, since he was already married to somebody else.

In general, the truth is somewhere in-between. A practice or business can actually do enough marketing to get by, even without measuring ROI. However, their growth will be extremely limited because they are proceeding with the "shotgun" approach to marketing. They are shooting their marketing blindly all over the place, without knowing if it is hitting the target, but hoping at least to get a piece of that target.

You have to wonder, though, how much more profits and how many more new customers they would have, if they would only take the time to track their marketing and measure their campaign ROIs by ramping up their ROI Power.

Think of it this way: What if Dan the dentist never took X-rays of his patients' teeth and just treated them by what he could see by looking in their mouths? Imagine how many problems he would miss, problems that would worsen because he had not identified them when they were easily treated.

ROI measurements provide exactly the same function as X-rays do for dental treatment. It allows you to identify and solve problems quickly. Even more than that, it allows you to uncover lucrative opportunities for sales conversions and lead generation.

Consider the stories of Dan and Larry the next time you are brainstorming your next marketing moves. Remember, the more you can learn about your campaigns, the more cost-effective and profitable your marketing campaigns become.

It all comes down to three letters—ROI—that brings us to our ROI Rule:

> ### *ROI Guy Rule*
> *If you want to marry Darla and have babies (or just make outstanding profits) Listen to her about ROI!!!*

Section Two
Working with ROI Power

While ROI Power is mostly designed to energize your marketing, there are also many effective ways to "plug it in" to your actual work processes.

In this second section, we will analyze how you and your staff can relate to your customers, clients and/or patients in a more proactive way and realize a much better return from your investment of *time* spent interacting with them.

Your existing customers already know you and buy from you. You have already made it past the major hurdles with them. This section is all about how to take advantage of that fact and gain more sales from them, as well as provide more value *to* them

Chapter 5
"What Do You Want Out of Me?"

Training Your Staff and Yourself

Let us say your marketing did its job and a hot prospect wants to know more about your product or service. You have a lead who is incredibly interested in buying from you; however, he has a couple of questions. Unfortunately, he dials your number at the same time your receptionist steps out for a cigarette break, and forgets to turn on the voice mail system before leaving. The prospect waits on the line, ready to do business. Instead of being greeted by a person answering his call, or even a voice mail, what he gets is ringing. Ring. Ring. Ring, I could type out ten more "rings," but you get the idea. You are not making that sale today, or probably ever.

Here is an alternate scenario. Perhaps, as luck would have it, the generated lead calls *after* your receptionist's cigarette break. The receptionist says, in a tired voice, (it is 3:00 o'clock and the burrito she had for lunch is making her really, really sleepy), "Hi, so-and-so's office, may I help you?"

"Yes," the prospect says, "I'm really interested in such and such."

"Oh," says the receptionist. "Okay. That costs so-and so."

"Actually, I had a few questions first. Does it do thus and such? How long does it take?"

"Uh...I think it does that. Probably take a couple of weeks," yawns the receptionist.

Awkward pause.

"Could you find out for sure?"

"Um...I guess...hang on."

The receptionist puts the phone down on top of the desk—not on hold, and heads into your office to ask you the question. As it turns out, you are talking with someone else on another line. The receptionist waits, not indicating to you that it is important in any way. You hang up and she finally asks the question. You answer her quickly and think, "Haven't I already told her these things about five hundred times???" Meanwhile, she goes back and picks up the phone and discovers a dial tone. The receptionist shrugs and looks forward to another cigarette break. No skin off her teeth. The prospect who hung up? He has not lost anything either. He found someplace else to place his order.

Meanwhile, here is what you have lost: (a) a sale (b) potential future business (c) contact information (d) some impromptu marketing research on what campaign got the person to call in the first place and (e) a big dent in your overall ROI. You spent a lot of money on that campaign in order to attract potential buyers and all you have to show for it is a turned-off prospect who thinks you run a Mickey Mouse organization.

The last customer you should be losing is the one who is coming to you, ready to buy. That should be a no-brainer, unfortunately all too often we stop thinking about our business marketing at our own doorstep and we end up losing valuable revenues.

Here are two things that need to happen when you get this kind of call. First of all, when someone contacts you out of the blue about something you sell, you should say a little prayer of thanks to the business gods, because a red-hot lead just showed up on your doorstep (or in your email box or on your phone line). You inherited *the ideal sales opportunity:* a potential customer who is already interested in buying what you offer. To begin with, do not limit yourself to answering his or her questions; instead, ask some of your own.

For instance, you could ask:

- How did you hear about us?
- Why do you need our particular product or service?
- How can we best serve that need?

When you start a conversation with a lead, you begin to create an actual relationship. Key to a good relationship is raising the lead's comfort level.

The second huge glaring error is the fact that the receptionist never asked for the caller's contact information. Again, this is a red-hot lead. This is someone who is contacting you to express interest in whatever it is you sell. Don't you think it would be a great idea to get that person's name or at the very least, his email address for follow-up marketing?

Anyone in your business, including you, who receives a call from an interested prospect, needs to do the following:

1. Engage the caller personally
2. Get their name and contact information
3. Find out their needs and relate them back to how your business can meet them
4. Store the information accurately in the business's marketing software database

These sound like common sense but, like so many other marketing necessities, important and valuable phone techniques get forgotten in the day-to-day business routine. Other fires need to be put out, other tasks have to be finished and it is easy to forget to do the things that make you more money, get you more customers and grow your business.

Later in this book, I will talk about ways to automate these necessary tasks in such a way that you will not have to sweat them. However, even with such automation in place, there will occasionally be the need for the "human touch".

That is why this chapter's "ROI Guy Rule" is such a big one:

ROI Guy Rule

Every customer or lead interaction is a sales opportunity—NOT an inconvenience!

Why You Should Think Like A Car Dealer, Even If You Only Sell Hubcaps

When you walk onto a car lot, you know what is going to happen. One of the twelve or so salespeople pacing around the floor is going to approach you and ask if they can "help" you. You know that what they want to do is to "help" you decide that what you want to buy is their biggest, most expensive car. That hard sell is a reason many people do not like to walk onto a car lot. They do not like it!

If you are a doctor or lawyer, you do not want to turn away potential patients or clients by trying to hustle them when they come through the door. However, I am not talking about hard sell. I am talking about the basic idea that car dealers use to run a successful business. They crowd their lots with sales professionals who are trained to do what it takes to hook a customer.

Since businesses are supposed to make money, it makes sense that employees should be trained in how to make that happen; and yet, they are not. Even more importantly, you should be trained in that discipline, too.

I am going to talk a little more about creating the ideal customer experience and meeting their needs in the next couple of chapters. For now, however, let me get back to the idea of building relationships. There is the old saw that "people buy people" and it is totally true. If a customer or patient feels warm and welcome when they come through your door, chances are they are going to want to keep coming through it.

That kind of friendly experience is even more critical when it comes to a new potential customer. They are on the lookout to see how they are going to be treated from the get-go.

If you are making them feel insignificant or ignored, that is not going to make them jump at the chance to buy from you.

In other words, what you take away from the car dealers' approach is to engage people who call or come into your business. After all, they are coming to you with a reason and many folks are just too plain shy to articulate that reason properly. That is why you ask questions, without making it directly about selling.

Now, it is time to answer the question I posed in this chapter's title, "What do they want from me?" Or, in other words, what do your customers and leads want from you (and your staff)? This is easy to answer. They want a friendly, comforting exchange with someone with authority and knowledge in the expertise they are looking for. They want to feel they can trust whomever they are dealing with.

Let us talk about how we get all that done with some "ROI Power Plays." In all the chapters from here on out, we will end with proven tactics and strategies designed to boost your ROI. Here are the first ones:

ROI Power Plays: Taking Action to Improve Interaction

There are actually several ROI Power Plays that will improve both your staff's and your own conversations with current and potential leads that are both easy and affordable. Here are three of the best ones.

Get Professional Sales Training

You can bring in an expert for a one-day training seminar and/or even spring for a weekend seminar on how to improve the level of communication in your business. This is something that is not natural for most people but it can be learned. There are many valuable tricks and tips you can gain from these kinds of sales trainers that you can implement on a daily basis in your offices.

Create Phone Scripts

You can actually create or purchase scripts that will help your staff go in the right direction when speaking to leads and customers. The trick is for your staff person to make the interchange sound as natural as possible and not like they are reading from a script. That means you should encourage them to capture the idea of the scripted words but to put them into their own words as much as possible.

Here is a sample of a script that can be used by someone who works for a dentist to find out if the patient was happy with his or her experience at the practice:

Staff: Hi, this is [Your Name] from [Name of Dental Practice]. Is this [Name of Patient]?

PATIENT RESPONSE

Staff: Hi [*Name of Patient*], I was calling to follow up on your recent treatment here and make sure that everything worked out well for you. Were you happy with the treatment and [*Name of Dentist*]'s care so far?

If there is a problem...

Staff: I'm very sorry to hear that. What can we do to improve things?

PATIENT RESPONSE

Staff: Thank you so much for telling me about this situation. We want to make sure everyone has a good experience and we will try to make things work better for you in the future. Is it okay if I follow up after your next appointment to see if your experience was better?

PATIENT RESPONSE

Staff: Thank you for your time and have a good day/evening.

If there's not a problem...

Staff: Thank you very much for your feedback. Hearing from patients like you helps us to do everything possible to provide the best possible care. Thanks for your time and we look forward to seeing you at your next appointment.

Record and Review

Businesses that use my marketing systems are set up to record every incoming call to their offices. Why? If conversion rates start to decline from leads inquiring about a product or service, we can listen to the calls and pinpoint problems.

This is not meant to be a punitive process for those who handle the phones at an office. It is meant to be a learning experience and you cannot learn unless you actually hear what you are doing wrong.

When you actually listen to yourself, you will be surprised how obvious the problem might be. It could be as simple as the tone of your voice or the language you are using. Whatever the case, reviewing recordings of your calls is an invaluable tool to use when working with receptionists and others who answer the phones.

Dealing with lead walk-ins and phone calls is really an art, an art that can pay off big for your business. By properly training yourself and your staff, you can transform everyone into an unofficial sales staff (or make them official and hand out badges or something, whatever works!).

Most of you reading this are business or practice managers/owners who spend a great deal of effort, not to mention a good deal of money, creating marketing campaigns that are designed to generate interested leads. Generating those leads is only half the battle. You may have made them interested in buying from you, but once they actually have contact with you, their decision can still go either way. That is why you and your staff should always be fully prepared to "close the sale." Put the systems in place that will allow everyone to handle leads with ease and you will be the richer for it!

Chapter 6
As Long as They're Breathing

Creating Customer Experiences that Last a Lifetime
In the last chapter, I talked about how to deal with interested leads in a way that would make converting them to customers relatively easy.

In this chapter, I am moving to the next stage, that is, making sure your current customers do not go anywhere else to buy what you already sell. Let us face the facts; you are not the only one trying to get new clients or patients, even if it is at the expense of someone else. Your competition is doing the same thing, day after day and if they succeed, it could be at your expense.

That is why the "normal" guidelines of good customer service are not good enough anymore. This is especially true if your ultimate goal is creating customer loyalty that lasts a lifetime as it should be.

Sit down and do the math. Add up what a good customer earns you per year and then multiply that by the average life span of a customer. The number will probably make your eyes pop wide open!

When you go above and beyond to show your customers you care, you make them feel happy and maybe even excited to come back for more. I know of one fellow who did just that and made a billion dollars as a result!

If the Shoe Fits...
In 1999, Tony Hsieh was an Internet entrepreneur who was talked into investing in an online shoe company, Zappos. He was not crazy about the idea, but after looking at the numbers, he saw potential. When one year later, the dot.com bubble burst, and fortunes were being lost, his company was desperate for a direction.

Hsieh decided to go beyond being an investor and became the Co-CEO. Quickly, he decided the direction he wanted to take the company. Zappos would be all about customer service. While most companies directed their phone operators to get people off the line as quickly as possible in order to sell to as many leads as possible, Zappos employees were told to take as much time as a caller needed. Further, they were directed to send them to the competition if Zappos did not have what they were looking for.

Relentlessly they searched for the right people to work for the company to ensure they could deliver the crazy-high level of customer service. Applicants for a position at Zappos not only had to have the right qualifications, they also were interviewed to make sure they could fit into the Zappos culture.

After the two-stage interview process, the new hire then had to go through a four-week training period. At the end of the four week process, they were offered $2000 to quit. In the opinion of Hsieh, if the employee felt Zappos was the right place for them, they would turn down the money. If they did not care about working at Zappos, they would gladly pocket the money and quit. They would then be free to get another job somewhere else.

That is how Zappos became a company that was all about providing the best customer experience imaginable and it just happened to sell shoes. The goal of providing the best possible customer service worked like gangbusters. Hsieh wanted to hit a billion dollars in annual revenue by 2010. He achieved his goal in 2008, two years early! This is what creating the ultimate customer experience did for him, what can it do for you? Here is a hint...

Don't Do What You're Supposed to Do

Wait, what? Did I just say to NOT do what you are supposed to do? Yes, I did, but with an explanation! You are probably already wondering how to create the "ultimate customer experience" in your specific business. How far do you have to go? Do you have to give back rubs? If your business is massages, then yes, otherwise, probably not.

More seriously, you may think you need to do things like: answer and address complaints promptly, be friendly and courteous to customers, guarantee your work, and be transparent about costs. You know everything a business is supposed to do for their customers. Except what I am saying is do what you are not supposed to do. It is no longer enough to provide traditional "good" customer service. Why? Customers today already expect that level of service and if they do not get it, they get upset about it. If everyone is delivering the basics of good customer service then nobody stands out and that is why you have to do what you are not supposed to do. I certainly do not mean that in a bad way such as dumping a bucket of cold water over your customers' heads or calling them names. You are definitely not supposed to do those things (and I surely hope you do not, or if you do, at least video it and put it on YouTube, so I can watch!).

Of course what I mean is to do what you are not supposed to do in a good way. Let me give you two real-life examples:

An 89-year old Pennsylvania man was snowed in around the holidays and his daughter was concerned he was not going to have enough food to make it to the New Year. She called all the area stores she could think of to find one that would deliver, but nobody would. Finally, the local Trader Joe's said that while they do not normally deliver, they would make an exception in this case. Not only did the store employee take the order, but he also suggested items that would work for the man's special low-sodium diet. By the way, she was not charged for the food order!

A New Jersey Starbucks refused to honor a man's 10% Starbucks gold card discount because they were not a corporate-owned store. Since they were only a franchise location, they felt they were under no obligation to do so. The customer tried to cancel his drink order, but, since the drink had already been brewed, the employee refused to refund his six dollars. The guy called the corporate offices to complain. The corporate representative insisted on mailing him a $50 SBux Card that he could transfer onto his Gold Card.

In both cases, the businesses in questions did not do what was customary. To quote the happy customer from the Starbucks story, "They pulled out all the stops and went way beyond what they needed to." In other words, they did what they were *not* supposed to do. When you are running a business, you are not supposed to over-deliver to that extent. Nevertheless, when you do, you get a reputation, an awesome reputation. I know about these incidents and so do a lot of other people. As a result many people think more highly of Trader Joe's and Starbucks. Here is another ROI Guy Rule to remember:

ROI Guy Rule

Memorable customer service means going beyond business as usual and delivering incredible results!

Becoming an "Everyday Sensation

The only problem with the above approaches is, you cannot afford to give everybody who walks in a $50 gift card and you cannot afford to deliver your products for free on a regular basis. It is great to do something like that once in a while, it is what I like to call a "Hero Moment" because it usually generates some decent buzz and it is nice to give back like that when you can afford to.

It is important that we go beyond the Hero Moment and be an Everyday Sensation. Here is an example of what I mean: There is a Mexican restaurant our family regularly goes to and our four sons get really, really excited about it when we mention we are thinking about eating there. Why? At the entrance there is a counter with a small bowl and in that small bowl is a pile of individually wrapped Starburst candy pieces. When we say the name of the restaurant, the boys do not really hear it. They only hear "FREE CANDY! FREE CANDY! FREE CANDY!" over and over in their brains. Okay, I admit it, I do too.

Like most parents we only allow them to have one or two pieces of the candy. Additionally, there is a host or hostess always present to oversee any attempt at Grand Candy Larceny. The cost to this restaurant is, perhaps a couple dollars a day, at most. There is no way to really calculate the ROI from those couple of dollars, but I am sure my kids are not the only ones who nag their parents to go there!

The challenge for every business owner is to think of simple things such as the candy dish that other places are not doing and, which for the most part, are remarkably easy and affordable to accomplish.

Think about the traditional waiting room at a dentist's or doctor's office. All of us know that when we arrive for an appointment, there is a good chance we may end up sitting around for a half-hour or longer with nothing else to do but read and re-read a *People's* magazine from 2003. Not a great way to make a patient happy or make them feel good about returning for a follow-up appointment.

In today's world there are some medical professionals who have begun to set up little individual waiting rooms with internet access. While their patients wait they are able to surf the web or even get some work done. Others have even set up little spa areas, so their fortunate patients can get a facial or a back rub while waiting!

When you invest in your customers/patients in this way, you make them feel important. You send the message that their time matters as much as yours. It also provides a sense of caring for them while acknowledging that you understand waiting is a big inconvenience.

In other words, I am talking about putting in place an overall mindset, much like Zappos implemented, in which the customer comes first. Being human means we all tend to put our own interests ahead of others in many situations. When it is our business, we want it to be about us, but that is the opposite approach you should take toward your customers.

When you invest in the people who pay your bills, you invest in creating the lifetime loyalty I talked about. You also create a bedrock of ongoing business that keeps you afloat even when the economy might be threatening to sink everyone else.

Think about that dish of Starburst candies and think about how you can implement the spirit of that dish into your everyday business. When you and your staff start the day with your customers' wants and needs as your main order of business, you are investing in a lifetime of success, an ROI that keeps them coming through the door.

Here are a few ROI Power Plays along those lines:

ROI Power Plays: Becoming Customer-Centric

Walk Through Your Customer's Experience

Do a walk-through with your staff of the typical experience for anyone who comes into your place of business. Look at each area of the experience and look for ways to "up the ante." Those methods could be as simple as the candy dish or as complex as the mini-spa. The important thing is to take the time to focus on that experience. Get the thoughts of everyone who works for you from the perspective of their specific roles. For instance, your receptionist might have the most powerful ideas, because he or she is interacting with the public the most and can more clearly see where things could be improved.

Survey and Modify

Follow up with your clients after a visit or a purchase (especially if it was an expensive one!) and find out what they liked and, more importantly, what they did not like. This follow up can be a simple online survey you send them and encourage them to respond to by offering a special discount or an entry to a prize raffle. Or it could be a personal phone call from you or one of your staff.

While the personal touch is always nice, keep in mind that in actuality, your customers may be more honest in an anonymous online survey!

Hire Mystery Video/Shoppers

Hopefully, you have done the #1 ROI Power Play for this chapter and thought through the customer experience at your business to identify areas for improvement. This ROI Power Play literally lets you see the customer experience for yourself and is invaluable to fine-tuning or even making big fixes, to your operation.

Hiring a Video Mystery Shopper or Patient is an excellent idea. The mystery shopper or client will come into your place of business and secretly videotape their entire visit with a hidden video camera. Afterward, you and your staff will be able to review the entire tape and there will not be room for any excuses or justifications. If your business is not treating your customers in the best possible way, you will instantly see all the problems through the Video Mystery Shopper's footage.

Most people who work at a business see their own operation from inside a bubble. The day-in and the day-out running of a company often sees bad habits become ingrained as well as opportunities wasted for both the retention of current customers and the conversion of new prospects.

That is why the tape from a Video Mystery Shopper can be an awesome wake-up call. Maybe a customer is left waiting for fifteen minutes without anyone paying attention to them. Maybe questions are ignored, sales openings are missed, follow-up appointments are not pursued, or maybe your staff comes off as plain rude in some instances. Another bonus of viewing the tape might be that you can easily spot what the equivalent of my favorite restaurant's "dish of Starbursts" should be. Even better, maybe you can be as lucky as one of my dentist clients was, and have the Mystery Shopper actually be so impressed, he becomes a regular patient!

Here is another advantage of the Video Mystery Shopper, you and your staff will actually know in advance this person is going to show up at some point, only you will not know when. That means all of you are going to be extra-careful to treat your customers right, after all, you do not want to look bad on video!

Use the Personal Touch

When you are in a personal care-based business such as a chiropractor, dentist, doctor, etc., you should continually find ways for you and your staff to connect with your patients on a more personal basis. Send a card or email on their birthdays to wish them a great day. When you hear about a special event in their lives, say, a 30th wedding anniversary, a child's graduation or even a death in the family, send a personal message appropriate to that event.

Finally, with the help of your staff, create "cheat sheets" about each of your patients. Have the names of their spouses and children, and other pertinent information to review before they come in. Eventually, you will not need a cheat sheet, but in the meantime, they will be pleased that you remembered and asked them about their families.

When a customer has an amazing experience doing business with you, he or she will want to keep doing business with you. When you invest in them, they will continue to invest in you and that is a ROI you will be able to count on for decades to come!

Chapter 7
You Can Always Get What You Want

Identifying, Creating and Meeting Needs with Upselling

"Do you want fries with that?" That question has become kind of a punch line for our times, a joke you throw around when somebody asks you for something. However, do not forget where the line came from. It came from a time before the fast food franchises had combination meals. Yes, back in the Stone Age, before Happy Meals learned how to smile. Back in those prehistoric days when you rode your dinosaur up to the drive-through window, ordered a burger, and the employee would ask, "Do you want fries with that?"

This is a golden example of the principle of upselling. When you are asked if you want fries, it is because you did not order them. You may not have wanted them, but perhaps you did and forgot to order them. Or maybe you were not even thinking about fries and suddenly, they sounded good. Whatever the case, if you answered by saying, "Why, yes, I do want fries with that!", then the burger place just made a sale it otherwise would have lost. Upselling is common sense for a business. Unfortunately, most businesses do not do it or do not understand it enough to do it well.

In this chapter, I am going to talk about how to successfully implement upselling within your business and get the best shot at obtaining the highest ROI from each customer who buys from you.

Tapping Into Needs and Wants

In the past few chapter I have done a lot of talking about how to create great experiences for each customer/client/patient you serve. So far, the emphasis has been on you and your staff and what you can do to make those who buy from you feel valued and important.

Next, we will now delve deeper into your customers' consciousness to discover what they *need* as well as what they *want* from you. To do that, you have to understand the difference between the two.

A *need* is something customers feel, at that moment, they MUST have. It is what might drive a customer your way when they ordinarily would have avoided buying from you. For example, when your car's gas tank is on "E", you NEED to get to the nearest gas station. No matter what brand of gas it is selling, you pull right up to the nearest pump. If your tank was not registering empty, you would have driven right by it.

Now the thing is, that need has done a lot of heavy lifting for the gas station. It has brought you in as a customer, without them having to spend a dime on marketing. They know that. They also know that, while you stand there, pumping the gas that you NEED, you might decide you WANT a cup of coffee or a soda to drink. That is the reason why so many service stations now have mini-marts. Since the need for gas is bringing in so many customers, it is a waste not to try to upsell them other things that they might WANT while they are on the road. A "want" is something you would like, but not necessarily need. Impulse buying is usually based on "wants," not "needs."

Remember why that gas station has a mini-mart and think to yourself, are you making available WANTS to your customers when they come in for a NEED? If you are wondering how to get that done, let us look at two different scenarios where a sudden need drives a customer into a business:

Case #1: Larry, the lawyer, has been avoiding the dentist. One morning, he wakes up with a toothache so bad he cannot think straight and he quickly calls to make an appointment ASAP.

Case #2: Samantha, the sales manager, ignores all the coupons she gets emailed from the local office supplies store. One evening, while finishing an important project at home, she discovers her printer is out of ink, and rushes to that same store before closing time.

Those are the *needs* and, as you can see, needs do not allow for procrastination. A need is something you need NOW! Larry and Samantha immediately went to the place that could help them meet their individual needs quickly.

This dynamic duo, like most people, also has some wants they have not attended to. These are things they have thought about, but had not considered a huge priority. Let us look at what they are:

Case #1: While at the dentist, Larry gets a good look at his teeth in the mirror and remembers having thought earlier in the week that they looked a little dull and dingy. He makes a remark about their appearance to the dental assistant, who is setting him up for treatment.

Case #2: While at the store, Samantha remembers she has been meaning to buy a new keyboard for her home office. The one she has is so old; she can no longer read half of the letters on the keys. The office supplies store is huge and she is not sure where they have keyboards on display.

We have a couple of cliffhangers here, folks. Which way are these stories headed? Are we going to have two Happy Endings? Hang on and I will tell you.

Case #1: The dentist treats Larry's problem successfully and Larry leaves. He was going to bring up getting a whitening treatment of some kind, but decided that it would probably take too long and he had briefs to get done.

Case #2: Samantha finds the ink cartridge she needs for her printer and takes it to the check-out counter. The cashier silently scans the cartridge; Samantha swipes her credit card, and leaves the store, without a keyboard. She does not have time to look for it because she is facing a deadline with a work project.

For everyone concerned, we have two unhappy endings. Larry and Samantha missed out on getting something each of them wanted and both businesses lost out on making an extra sale.

These stories did not have to end this way. We could easily have had happy endings that would leave everyone feeling better. This is another way that stories could have gone:

Case #1: The dental assistant mentions to the dentist, that Larry seems to think his teeth are not as bright as they should be. The dentist, as he is treating Larry, mentions that they have a whitening procedure they can do if Larry has an extra fifteen minutes. Larry, whose mouth is filled with dental apparatuses, replies enthusiastically, "Wskjhbrrhhb!" Luckily, the dentist is good at interpreting a mouth-full-of-stuff English. Larry leaves a little later pain-free, with a whiter smile and plenty of time to get his work done.

Case #2: At the check-out counter, the cashier asks Samantha if she was able to find everything okay. Samantha says, "Oh, I

wanted a new keyboard, but I really don't have time today..."
The cashier smiles and says, "I can have somebody get you
one of the more popular ones; it is on sale today. Did you
want a wireless one?" Samantha nods and says, "That would
be wonderful." She goes home, hooks up her new keyboard
and happily finishes up her report, no longer having to guess
where the "a" and the "e" keys were.

For those of you who think upselling is something sleazy, here is this
chapter's ROI Guy Rule:

ROI Guy Rule:

*Upselling helps your customers as much as it helps you.
If you are not doing it, why not?*

Secrets of Upselling

Upselling does not mean you have to be obnoxious and pushy with your
customers. As a matter of fact, that is the last thing you want to be because
that kind of approach sets off all kinds of alarm bells for consumers. They
know when they are being hustled. Even if you are offering something with
genuine value, they might not trust that it is worthwhile, simply because you
are trying so hard to get them to buy it. The reality is you actually have to
put very little effort into it. Upselling means you are meeting customer
wants and needs that they may have forgotten about, or may not even have
known they had (we will get to that one later). Upselling is more a matter
of making them aware that you can provide the goods or services, if they
are interested. Again, you are providing more value to them, while, at the
same time, realizing more revenue from them.

Larry wanted whiter teeth. Samantha wanted a new keyboard. They
were both busy people who did not want to waste time on getting these
things that were not necessities at the moment. Larry got what he wanted
when the dental assistant actually listened to what he was saying and knew
enough to mention it to the dentist. Samantha got what she wanted when
the cashier asked if there was anything else she was looking for, and then
made it incredibly easy for her to get it.

The secrets behind both upsells? I am glad you asked.

Secret #1: The Upselling Was Done Through Normal Conversation

In both cases, there was not a real sales pitch involved. Questions were asked: "Do you want a quick and easy teeth whitening procedure?" "Were you able to find everything okay?" Ensuing sales followed from their responses. The original upsell question we mentioned at the beginning of this chapter, "Do you want fries with that?" is along similar lines. The fast food guy did not suddenly start yammering about how tasty and great their fries were and try to pressure the customer into buying them.

Simple conversation works best. If the customer is not responsive to your suggestion, then drop it. No point in going on, unless there is another piece of information that might be helpful to them.

Secret #2: The Upselling Was Directed at Existing "Wants"

Nobody forced Larry and Samantha to buy anything they did not already want. In fact, both businesses empowered them to get what they wanted in as convenient a manner as possible. No sales person pushed them to consider something they did not want to hear about.

Secret #3: The Staff Was Trained to Identify and Act on Customer Desires

The dental assistant, in our "happy ending," had been coached to listen to what patients had to say about their dental health and appearance and to let the dentist know about another service they might want.

The same is true with our office supplies store "happy ending". The cashier had been trained to ask all customers if they had found everything they were looking for, just like employees are doing at big chain stores. Even though that is a very general inquiry, it is still effective, especially for someone like Samantha who did not have time to search the store for an item she did not need to have at that very minute.

Upselling is very frequently as effortless as I have portrayed it in those stories. The hard part is always getting the customer into your place of business (or buying from your website, if you are a virtual merchant). Once the customer is there, you need to keep your eyes and ears open to identify something else he or she might want or need. In the virtual world, you need to program your website to display products that are similar to, or that complement, the products they are browsing, like Amazon does.

If you do not take these simple upselling steps, you risk leaving money on the table. Also, customers might not be as happy as they could have been, simply because they did not get everything they wanted. For instance, the Samantha who left without a keyboard might have complained to her friends that things are hard to find at that particular store, whereas the

Samantha who got her keyboard, might rave about how helpful that store's personnel were.

Upselling is simply good customer service. To be honest, it is obviously good business as well.

The Next Level of Upselling

The upselling scenarios I discussed were pretty much that easy, but sometimes successful upselling can get a little trickier. For instance, what if that fast food guy asked, "Do you want fries with that?" and you did not know what fries were?

Many times businesses will sell products and services that people do not know about. That does not mean the customer would not want them if they knew about them. That is why educating customers about other things you sell is key to successful upselling. When McDonalds, Burger King ,or other fast food restaurants, are selling a new food item, they make sure and show you what it looks like (or what the fantasy version of it looks like, to be more accurate). There is a big tasty picture of it on the drive-through menu, on the interior menu and even on special cards placed on their dining tables. They want you to see the new food sensation and say, "Wow that looks yummy, what is that?" and then, of course, order it. Too good for fast food? Okay, let me sit you down at a fancy restaurant. After your server has told you his or her name, the first thing they do is begin their memorized spiel, "Tonight, we have a few specials..." Then the server will describe those specials in delicious detail, including the way they are cooked and the kind of sauce they are served in. The point is people cannot decide whether they want to buy something until they know (a) what it is, and more importantly, (b) the benefit of it to them.

For instance, a dental practice may install new technology that allows them to fit and manufacture a new dental crown in one visit, rather than the old-school way of taking two or three appointments to get it done. Convenience is a big selling point to today's busy consumers, therefore, it is worth letting your patients know about it.

Here are five easy ways, without getting into costly advertising, to educate your customers about special products/services they might like, but may not know enough about:

Signage

A simple sign on the premises, generally on a wall near the receptionist or cashier, can often intrigue a customer. For instance, for our above dentist, the sign could read "Ask us about our new one-hour crown service."

Email and Direct Mail
If you are beginning to sell a product or service that you think is particularly appealing, an email or direct mail campaign educating your customer base about the new offering could be called for.

If it is something new, people appreciate being informed about it.

Website and Social Media
When products or services need a little more explanation, publishing regular articles about them on your website is a great educational method.

The important thing is to spread the word about these articles through Twitter, Facebook and whatever other social media avenues your business uses, so potential customers know to check them out.

Personnel
I am back to the guy asking you if you want fries. Like him, your people should be trained to mention additional products or services that customers might like, but might not be aware of.

If you have regular customers or patients that you and your staff have good relationships with, you may even know who might be in the market for a certain something you sell, and start a conversation with that person about it.

Informational Products
This is something I am going to cover in more detail in the next chapter. Suffice to say, you can get a double sale out of this category.

You can sell the informational product and sell the service the product is about. Pretty good!

What You Don't Know About Your Customers
Let me share one last upselling scenario involving, once again, our favorite fast food guy (who is due for overtime after the workout I have given him in this chapter). This time, he does not ask if you want fries. He does not ask you because you stride confidently up to the counter and order a burger and fries without him having to say a word! Now the guy looks a little uncomfortable because this place does not sell fries. Also imagine how much money they are missing out on because they do not carry a product that many customers would buy.

The focus in this kind of upselling is not on educating your customers, but educating yourself: What might your customers happily lay down a few dollars for that you are not providing to them? In other words, are you depriving yourself of any upselling opportunities? You should find out. There are two primary ways of doing that:

Survey your competition.
Sometimes companies providing the same products or services are offering things that you do not. The result is that you do not realize that they have taken away many of your customers! Keeping tabs on what the competition is selling is a good way to see if you are keeping pace with the marketplace, and how you might make a few more dollars.

Survey your customers.
If you want to know what your customers want, ask them. You can do that with a simple formal survey, or through one-on-one conversations. Look for a consensus on what might be missing or what could be a great addition to your existing offerings; then add them.

In this chapter I have covered three methods of creating upselling opportunities:
1. Provide "Wants" when a customer comes in with a "Need"
2. Educate customers about your other products/services
3. Identify customer wants and needs that you are not currently providing

Here are a few ROI Power Plays, one for each method, that will help you ramp up your revenue (simply by giving your customers what they want!):

ROI Power Plays: Attaining Upselling Success

Sell "Wants" Related to Your Expertise
If you have a private practice and someone comes to see you with a "need," make sure you are able to supply them with a "want" related to that need.

For example, if you are an eye doctor, you might want to sell a line of eye washes, or other optical products that you trust, at the front desk. Similarly, if you are a dentist, you can do the same with dental products.

When patients come in for your specific service or product, they are already in a mind frame to buy products that align with your specialty. If you are selling these products, you are tacitly endorsing them. Since you are the expert, the patient will want to buy what you recommend and be motivated to purchase them from you. (A word of warning: make sure you are selling quality products that you genuinely trust or you risk tarnishing your reputation.)

By the way, this upselling strategy is not limited to doctors. It is about focusing on providing additional products/services that align with your core business.

Let Testimonials Tell Your Tale

When it comes to educating your customers about a product/service, see if you can gather some testimonials from other customers who have bought them and prominently feature them singing your praises online. It is more credible to have a third party talk how much they liked and benefitted from your product or service.

Put Yourself (and Your Staff) in Your Customers' Shoes

Take an hour or so with your staff and do the following exercise: Pretend all of you are customers of your own business. Hopefully, you have a staff of people of varying ages, genders and backgrounds. A varied staff will provide valuable feedback because everyone will have a slightly different perspective on this exercise. This is what you want each person to focus on: *"If I were a customer of this business, what might I want to buy that is not currently being offered?*

Then ask yourselves questions like the following:

- What additional products or services would be most convenient for customers to buy while they are here?
- What would be the most useful product for them to buy?
- What brings customers into our business? What are they looking for and what might they not be finding at present?
- What extra products or services, perhaps not related to our core business, might they still want when buying from us? Think about the gas station selling drinks and snacks, obviously, those have nothing to do with the purpose of the service station, but in many cases, they drive most of the revenues (just as popcorn and Coke pays the rent at movie theatres!).

Upselling can up your revenues dramatically, if you implement the right processes in the right way. Remember, never be too pushy in presenting other possible purchases. If you want to upsell with success, always make it a natural part of the customer experience.

Chapter 8
Talk Doesn't Have to Be Cheap

Creating Informational Products That Help You Sell

Have you ever been up in the middle of the night with insomnia and turned to the TV for some relaxing relief? If so, you might have been shocked to find that many of your favorite channels had been "kidnapped" by pseudo-programs that promise you the secrets to rock-hard abs, softer skin, and awesome cookware for the kitchen; not to mention the ones that tell you how to buy a better bra, get rid of belly fat or have incredible sex more often.

Basically, the solution to every conceivable problem can be found on these channels in the wee hours of the morning. The only catch is that the shows do not give you what they advertise. Obtaining the real solution requires you to purchase their product. (The good news is you can usually get two of them for the price of one; they merely double the shipping and handling fees!)

Obviously, I am talking about infomercials. These are shows produced by companies who want to sell their products to the viewers. They pay the cable channels to air them. Presumably, they sell enough of their stuff by educating viewers about the benefits they can realize by yanking out their credit card, making a call and placing an order, all before their spouses awaken and wonder what they are doing at 4:00 a.m.!

For a moment, think about the costs involved in creating these half-hour or hour-long shows. The company has to have a script written, hire a TV crew and rent a studio, as well as buy 400 barrels of caffeine for their hosts to drink during the actual taping. Not to mention, they still have to edit the show, and put in the music and titles. When all these things are done, they still have to buy time on multiple channels in order for the shows to actually air. All these things need to happen before they have sold even one item from the infomercial!

We might laugh at these infomercials when we happen across them while channel-surfing, but there is nothing funny about the bottom line. By

2014, infomercials are expected to be grossing around $174 billion per year. Yes, *billion*.

Here is this chapter's ROI Guy Rule:

ROI Guy Rule

Informational products sell big-time and can also sell YOU big-time

---

In other words, informational products are not only a great sales tool, they can also raise your prestige level more than a few notches, if you do them right. No matter what business you are in, you can take advantage of their benefits.

The ROI Power of Informational Products

I am not suggesting you take on anything like producing your own spectacular hour-long infomercial. Frankly, that is not necessary and for most of you, not practical or profitable.

However, it is easy to create your own professional informational product, one that makes you proud, instead of cringe. I repeat, most businesses can benefit from them. If you are a doctor, you can create a DVD on your specialty. If you are a dentist, you can create a special report on cosmetic procedures. If you are a personal injury lawyer, you can prepare an eBook on what to do if you are injured in an accident.

Maybe you are not that kind of professional, perhaps you sell products. For example, if you are an EBay seller who offers Barbie dolls from the past and present, you could create a mini-history of the toy. Or if you sell sports memorabilia, you could do a PDF featuring the ten biggest-selling sports souvenirs in history.

In other words, no matter what you do, there is probably an angle you can use to create an informational product that will be interesting to your current customers and could attract new ones.

Creating informational products bring with them several built-in business advantages:

You demonstrate your expertise.

No matter what your business might be, people want to be able to trust that you know what you are doing (obviously, this is particularly important if you are a medical or legal professional). By creating your own informational product, you showcase your knowledge of your specialty.

You reach a new audience.
If you are offering your product for free, many people will be interested in the information you are sharing and will watch, listen or read about your informational product. If the product is well-crafted, it could motivate them to learn more about you and finally, make a purchase from you.

You indirectly advertise what you are selling.
Go back to the example of the informational product I suggested for a personal injury lawyer, an eBook about what to do when involved in an accident. Obviously, in that eBook, the lawyer can talk about what an attorney does for a client in this situation and why it is important to have one representing you. If the informational product is impressive, then that would be reason enough for the reader to call him if he becomes involved in an accident or to recommend him to a friend or family member who is looking for a personal injury lawyer.

You build your brand.
A positive brand is important to any business. Having custom-made and professional informational products boosts your brand to the next level. You look like you know more and that you do more than the competition. When you write your own book or create your own DVD, you immediately look like one of the "big boys."

Informational Product Options
There many different ways to get your information out there. Here are a few of the most popular ones with ways to approach them.

eBook
You can easily create a short eBook (twenty to forty pages) that will give your reader solid information, without having to write the sequel to *War and Peace*. Remember to write in simple, clear language, with short paragraphs and chapters, and to make it accessible to the majority of people who might want to read it. Even if you are a doctor or a lawyer, *especially* if you are a doctor or a lawyer, you want to avoid complex jargon that readers either will not understand or will be put off by.

Special Report/White Paper
This is similar to the eBook idea, but even shorter (ten to twenty pages maximum). It should be in a PDF format that can be easily downloaded

from the internet. Actionable content is best in these kinds of pieces, meaning advice the reader can easily and quickly implement. Think *"The 10 Best Ways to..."* or *"The 7 Things You Should Do If..."* as the type of title concepts you should explore to grab a prospect's attention.

Online Video

You can make a series of instructional videos on some area of your expertise and post them on YouTube, Vimeo or if you prefer, limit them to your own website. This is an especially good approach if you have to demonstrate something visually (for example, if you are a martial arts instructor).

DVD

A longer video (twenty to sixty minutes) can be placed on DVDs that you can either sell or send out as part of a marketing campaign. If you have to visually demonstrate a product or service, or simply share some knowledge that requires a heavy visual component, this is the best way to go.

CD

If you are more comfortable being heard rather than being seen, a CD is easy to create. Simply get a decent recording program and record it directly onto your computer or laptop. Many people listen to CDs as they drive so this is not as outdated a concept as it might seem at first. By the way, a podcast can accomplish the same goals.

All of these types of informational products have their various pros and cons. Choosing which one to create depends on what you need to accomplish with it, who your audience is, and what plays best to your talents. You may be best at writing, therefore you may prefer to stick to special reports and eBooks. Perhaps you would prefer to display your great personality by performing in front of the camera. Or you may simply want to read the information and create a CD.

Whichever format you choose, make sure it is professional enough to help your image, not hurt it. For instance, you do not want to create a video that looks like a hostage video, shot under bad lighting with a less-than-professional camera. If you do not write well, do not publish an eBook that does not make sense or is filled with spelling or grammatical errors.

If you need help creating an informational product, get it. Elance.com is full of good, affordable writers who will be able to communicate your knowledge in a very readable way, as well as designers who can format a special report or eBook and make it look like a polished, finished work. If you need help shooting a video, contact a local videographer who has some experience (ask to see his or her reel first, so you can evaluate their work).

The whole point of an informational product is that it should look as professional as possible. If you are going to make one, make it right, to realize the best ROI from it!

To Sell or Not to Sell?

Once you have decided to create an informational product, the next question is whether you should sell it or give it away.

To be honest, it is almost always best to give away informational products in order to promote what you are really selling. Your costs are minimal in creating and storing an informational product. Most of them are digital files that can easily be kept on your computer then distributed for free through downloads on your website.

Sometimes, however, selling is the right way to go. For example if you were a fitness instructor who had gotten a lot of requests for a video version of one of your one-hour workouts. Providing a one-hour workout DVD and selling it in your fitness studio makes perfect sense. Clients are already accustomed to paying for CD's and would recognize the value of being able to purchase additional workout videos.

In the case of a special report, a short video or even an eBook, you are often better served by using these products as "lead generators." For example, you may want to add more names to your marketing database. By offering a free eBook to everyone who leaves a name and email address in your opt-in form on your website, you are providing a good motivator to encourage people to give up their contact information.

Whether you charge for your informational product or not, will really depend on how sophisticated it is, how long it is, and how much value it is delivering. Here is a good rule of thumb: if it is information you would not mind sharing in a general conversation with someone, it is a giveaway. If it is information you would not feel comfortable giving away to a customer or client for free, then you should not make it a give-away.

Suppose, for instance, you are a nutritionist, you might not have a problem listing the "7 Kinds of Foods You Should Be Eating Every Day." On the other hand, you would not want to share a complete dietary regime that could be used without seeing you.

Creating a Viable Informational Product

There are some important things to keep in mind as you are creating your informational product, to make sure you realize the best ROI possible from it. Jim Edwards, who co-authored *How to Write and Publish Your Own eBook...in as Little as 7 Days* gives these top 5 tips that are critical to take on board:

- **Niche it.** Aim your product at a well-defined group that will want it, rather than trying to make something that suits everyone in the world. Dentists, for example, would create a different informational product for teenagers (probably content about braces) then they would for seniors (where implants would be the prime topic).

- **Solve a problem**. This is a big one and goes hand-in-hand with making sure you're giving the reader or viewer actionable content. The more intense the problem, the more your target audience (those who suffer from the problem) will want your product.

- **Provide a sample**. This applies if you're selling the product for money. By giving those who might buy it a look at a portion of it (think of how Amazon.com lets you view a certain number of pages of a book before you buy), consumers can better decide if they want to have it.

- **Be entertaining**. Too often, an informational product can feel like going to school and we know how much fun that was. Add some humor or other entertaining factors to your presentation; it will increase positive word-of-mouth for you as well as your product.

- **Keep it evergreen**. Don't make too many references to top-of-the-moment pop culture sensations. Instead, create info products that will go the distance or, at most, need a little updating from time-to-time. Do this and you will have a product you can use for years to come.

Keep the above five factors front and center when creating your information product and you will be surprised at how effective it will end up becoming.

ROI Power Plays: Power-up Your Informational Products

Make a List of Topics for Your Informational Product

Before you begin putting together your informational product, make sure you have the best possible topic for it, one that will be magnetic to your hoped-for leads. To accomplish this, make a list of topics you might want to build your product around and ask staff members, and even some of your most loyal customers, what they would like your product to address.

After you have a list together, answer the following questions:

- Which topic would be of the most interest to potential clients, customers, or patients?
- Which topic would best showcase our expertise?
- Which has the best possibility of motivating sales from those who use it?
- Which would draw in the most people who are not already customers?
- What topic scores the highest? Build your product around it.

Let Your Customers Pick Your Presentation

If you are unsure whether to create a written, video or audio product, ask a few key customers which format they would prefer. If a consensus emerges, go with that format.

Distribute Your Product through Other Businesses

If you are creating a product designed to be given away, think about contacting other businesses you work with (not direct competitors) and see if they would help you distribute your product to their customers. This provides them with more value to deliver to their people and it allows you to spread your informational word beyond the confines of the reach of your business.

As a final note to this chapter, let me reveal a little secret that you may have already guessed: you are reading an informational product. While I have published some of what is contained within the pages as articles, chapters and blogs elsewhere, this is the first time I have put down this much of the hard-won knowledge I have accumulated about marketing ROI in one place.

Remember, you do not have to write a book as long as this in order to create an awesome informational product. Follow the advice in this chapter and you will have a lead generator that will work for you while you are sleeping!

Section Three
Marketing with ROI Power

In the last section, I talked about how to sell *inside* your business through interacting with customers, clients and/or patients by you and your staff.

In this section, I am going to take it outside. Do not worry, I am not talking about some kind of ROI Fight Club, I am a peace-loving guy. Instead, I am talking about how to craft and send out the perfect message that will attract new customers and swing word-of-mouth recommendations firmly in your direction.

Read on to examine basic marketing concepts and how you can specifically apply them to your business. Some of this content you may already know, but many you may not. In any case, it is important to understand all of it before you read Section 4, the section where the rubber really meets the road (and you get to discover how today's "Big Data" can make you big bucks!).

Now, without further ado, a jolt of ROI Marketing Power!

Chapter 9
"And You Are...?"

Building a Brand with a High ROI

You do not think you need a brand? Here is what you have to realize—whether or not you know it—you already have a brand, and it may not be one you like and it could be costing you money.

Daily, we are bombarded with information. In today's world, Information overload is not so much of a cliché as a way of life in the 21st century. What do our brains do to cope? We take complex people and situations and simplify them by categorizing and pigeonholing them for easy reference. For example, how might you remember some guy's wife? Oh yeah, she is the one with the big hair. Or how about his nephew, David? Right, he is the 13 year old kid who is already over six feet tall.

Of course, the people in these examples are definitely a lot more complex than those simple labels; however, it is the way you can remember them. Since they are probably not that important to your life, you file their most obvious characteristic in your head in order to recall them when you need to.

Your business is no different than that very tall nephew because it is not that important to those who are not regular customers. They will then remember your business by whatever stands out, and THAT is your brand.

If you are not in control of your brand, things can easily go wrong. Here are a couple examples of how people might "brand" a local business without the business knowing about it:

"Dr. So-and-So? Oh yeah, I had an appointment with her once and she kept me waiting an hour and a half."

"So-and-So's Auto Supplies? Oh yeah, that's the place that has the funny smell."

You see what I mean? Do you want your brand to be The Doctor Who Keeps Everybody Waiting Too Long? Or, worse, The Place That Smells Funny?

I did not think so, that is why it is important to be active in your branding efforts. You want to create the impression you want the public to have before they make one of their own!

Your Marketing Foundation

The foundation of all your marketing is your brand. It is why big companies like Coke and McDonalds build all their campaigns around a central brand concept: It unifies all the marketing so that the parts add up to more than the whole.

You may be thinking that you do not have the money to get your name out there, like a Coke or a McDonalds and you want to focus on marketing that brings in immediate dollars, not some long-term, pie-in-the-sky, pay-off.

Perhaps you think that, since I am the ROI Guy, I would agree with your assessment. After all, is branding really selling? For instance, what good does it do to plaster your face all across town so that everyone knows what you look like? Actually, it can do a whole lot of good. A prime example is Dr. Jonathan Zizmor. While you may not know who he is, if you live in New York City, you probably do. For years, Dr. Zizmor has plastered his ads all over the New York Subway system. Result? According to the website, TheGothamist.com, Dr. Zizmor is one of the hundred most recognizable New Yorkers, even though he is basically just another dermatologist.

Granted, he started advertising like this thirty years ago, but according to him, it did not take anywhere close to that long for it to start making him money. He said there was a big difference in his business the week after he started the first subway campaign which is why he has kept doing it for three decades.

Brands do make a difference, they can boost your ROI considerably and I can prove it.

The Branding Boost

Do you think people are more likely to buy from you if they believe you deliver more value than your competition? I think you will agree that the answer to that question is a big fat, "Yes." Trust is one of the leading motivators that cause prospects to make a purchase, and a known brand inspires more trust than an unknown one.

A *New York Times* article from March 25, 2011, demonstrates what happens when this theory is put to the test. The Harvard Business School showed the same article, an innocuous one about public finances in Greece, to a group of 700 people and asked them to rate its quality. Here is the twist: the article was presented in three different ways. When it was presented as coming from the prestigious magazine, *The Economist*, people gave it a quality rating of 6.9. When it was shown as a post from *The Huffington Post* website, people rated it at 6.1. Finally, when it was presented as old article from the internet, it got only a 5.4.

Same article with the same information. What made the difference in how it was regarded? This chapter's ROI Guy Rule has the answer.

ROI Guy Rule

When you sell the same products and services as your competition, your BRAND is most often WHY someone will decide to buy from you.

When you take the time and make the effort to build a positive lasting brand, it is an edge you can count on for years to come to work in your favor. If you do not have a brand working on your behalf, it can mean disaster.

Here is another case study that proves it. Grey Goose Vodka was subjected to a blind taste test against two much cheaper vodkas. Furthermore, the people who took part in the blind taste test were all enthusiastic Grey Goose fans. The result of the tasting? Grey Goose came in dead last! Judging from the test results, Grey Goose is making its money more because of its brand name recognition than from its actual product.

Here is another conclusive case study, this time on the kids' favorite, a McDonalds Happy Meal. Kids were fed a Happy Meal with the McDonalds wrapper and then the same meal with plain packaging. Guess what? The branded food that featured the Golden Arches was rated as being 77% tastier. That is a huge difference and it clearly shows that Ronald McDonald is not clowning around with his marketing.

I bet you can come up with similar examples fairly easily. For instance, how much do you pay for a Starbucks cup of coffee as opposed to one at a no-name coffee shop? More, right? You are willing to pay more because the Starbucks name is on the cup and you know and trust the Starbucks experience.

Branding does make a difference and does boost your ROI. If you can sell the same thing for more than the other guy, because you have built a name for yourself and/or your business, you are obviously going to see a direct financial benefit from your branding.

Branding creates credibility and leverages familiarity. You feel comfortable with a brand you like and you do not feel as comfortable buying something from someone with whom you have no experience. These are important factors that contribute mightily to purchasing decisions and only branding can create them.

A brand can increase sales and justify higher prices. When that brand is removed, it can cause the exact opposite effects and give a company a real pain in their ROI. For example, in 2006, the department store chain, Macy's, bought out the beloved Marshall Field stores in Chicago. They removed the huge outdoor Marshall Field sign and replaced it with their own name. Makes sense, right? Except store sales in Chicago plummeted. Macy's became the victim of a lot of negative press in the city from journalists who felt the company should have been more respectful of a time-honored brand that had meant a lot to Windy City residents. Macy's was seen as an interloper.

Breaking Down the Brand

David Ogilvy, the legendary advertising man, summed up a brand this way: "A brand is the intangible sum of a product's attributes, its name, packaging, history, reputation and the way it is advertised." What do those elements add up to? They combine to make a promise to your customers. People know that when they pull into the drive-through lane of a McDonalds or a Wendy's anywhere in America, the food is going to taste the same and cost the same. Even our subway dermatologist, Dr. Zizmor, is promising something in his branding: clear skin (and of course, the treat of seeing one of the hundred most recognizable faces in Manhattan).

Obviously, whatever "promise" you are creating with your branding has to be one people respond to, whether it is like the discount prices at Wal-Mart or the elegant jewelry of Tiffany's. Both businesses may seem worlds (or universes) apart, but they share a focused, powerful brand that appeals mightily to their particular niche.

Of course, a promise is not enough, or every politician in America would easily get re-elected. No, there has to be follow-through on the promise or consumers quickly reject the brand. If you pulled into an unfamiliar McDonalds and suddenly they were trying to sell you a Big Mac for $20, you probably would not trust the Golden Arches much longer.

Likewise, if you are a dentist promising painless treatment, and the person in your chair is screeching like a wounded hyena from your drilling, he is going to go out and tell everyone that you are misrepresenting your practice and that is going to irreparably harm your brand.

When you combine an attractive promise, with a consistent follow-through, you are building a strong brand ROI. That ROI is not only about money. Your brand is also delivering a strong Return on Investment in two key intangibles: *image* and *loyalty*.

When you create a positive image for your business or practice, it ends up selling itself. Positive images generate great word-of-mouth and "buzz". When your name is brought up, someone is liable to say, "Oh, I hear they are great," or "My brother swears by them." Both of those things are a lot better than anything involving a funny smell.

Not only that, but both of those statements create absolutely *free marketing*, as well as the most *powerful kind of marketing there is*. A recommendation by a trusted source is the best advertising in the world. After all, when you are marketing yourself, people are naturally wary; they know you want them to buy from you and would maybe stretch the truth a bit to make that happen.

Someone who promotes you to a friend or relative, however, is not getting anything out of the deal. Their intention is to take *care* of that friend or relative and make sure they go to someone who is good. That is why referral programs are awesome to have in place at your business.

The second great pay-off from branding is *loyalty*. When you promise and deliver over and over again, people return to do business with you again and again. Even if you do happen to screw up once, if you make good on the screw-up, you have probably built up enough good will to survive that mistake.

Measuring Brand ROI

So far, I have talked a lot about brand intangibles but now I am back to the question posed by the title of this chapter—*can you measure the real ROI of a brand?* In other words, can you actually *quantify* what having a great brand brings to your business or practice?

As a guy who devotes way too much time to thinking about this stuff (and who believes numbers do matter), I have come up with two methods to do just that. The first works to measure the worth of your *existing* brand and the second allows you to measure the impact of a *brand modification*. Both are essential to measuring the worth of your business and to making sure that your brand value stays strong.

Discover the Difference

Remember the Grey Goose blind taste test I discussed a little earlier? It is very easy to determine the ROI of their brand very quickly; it is the difference in price between their vodka and the cheaper ones. That cost difference is definitely a very credible number to determine how much their brand is adding to their bottom line.

There is a simple formula to this process:

Brand Cost - Non-brand Cost = Brand ROI.

This can work for virtually any business. For instance, if you were a chiropractor and had built-up a good name for yourself, you could check out a small chiropractic start-up and see what they were charging as opposed to your fees. The difference would be what your brand is delivering to you every day in added revenues. Of course, you may also find the small start-up is charging close to what you are charging and you should be able to increase your prices, based that information.

Track Your Branding Campaigns

I mentioned that Dr. Zizmor's business took a sharp upturn after he started "branding" himself with subway ads. Since that was thirty years ago, I am sure he was basing that observation when he noticed that more people were booking appointments with him.

It is a new century now and marketing measurement is definitely a different story. Thanks to marketing tracking systems, such as my own ROI Matrix which we will discuss in the last section of this book, we can measure to the penny, how much revenue a branding campaign such as Dr. Zizmor's generates. More importantly, you can check out how changes to your brand are affecting new customer conversions.

For example, you may be using marketing to advertise new offices, upgraded products and/or services, or to introduce a splashy new logo. In all those cases, you are modifying the brand a bit. What is the effect of what you are doing? Will prospects respond better to that modification or will it turn them off?

Tracking the branding campaign will tell the tale, especially if you are drilling deep with your data to monitor lead engagement (how long people stay on your website or how long will they watch your online video, for example). You will be able to see how many new leads you pick up, as well as how many your brand successfully converts to paying customers. Finally, you will see that all-important number, how much money your branding campaign brought in.

I hope you have seen in this chapter the very real value of creating a strong brand. Of course, you may still feel like it is more trouble than it is worth. Maybe you just want to sell, sell, sell. Or, simply do what you are good at and get paid for it. The problem with that logic is, if you are consistently in the same business day after day, you are consistently building a brand, whether you want to be or not. A reputation is being created, by your previous customers' experience with you, and it is best to be as much in control of that reputation as possible.

The other important issue to consider is that people love brands. Our marketing-mad society has convinced us that brands are to be trusted and used more often than not. When you go to buy something, odds are you will buy one with a logo slapped on it that you recognize. When you drive into a strange town and you need a meal, you will probably park your car in the lot of a chain restaurant that you are familiar with. Take a cruise down any large suburban shopping area and read off the names of the biggest stores, they are all chain stores with huge national brands.

ROI Power Plays: How to Supercharge Your Branding Make It Personal

Our friend, Dr. Jonathan Zizmor, the king of the New York City subway system, made his face his brand and it worked for him. People buy people, as the old truism goes, and that is doubly true when it comes to branding. It is the reason the head of a company will often do his or her own commercials, even though it is pretty clear they are not polished media performers.

Consider putting your face out there as the symbol of your brand. If you are comfortable in front of the camera and have a personality that connects well with people, let the public know who you are. They are more likely to buy from a person they like and trust than a nameless, faceless business.

Be Bold, But Don't Be Ridiculous
If you have ever seen the Will Ferrell Christmas comedy, *Elf*, you probably remember the scene where he goes into a small, grimy coffee shop with a sign in the window that says, "World's Best Cup of Coffee." Ferrell's character gets incredibly excited, runs in and yells to the guy working there, "You did it! Congratulations!" Of course, as it is made clear, Ferrell's character also knows almost nothing about anything and he is willing to believe that it is possible that this place actually does have the world's best cup of coffee. Clearly, nobody else would.

Your branding should not inspire a silly scene like this one, where you use an over-the-top slogan that is patently ridiculous. You might legitimately feel like you are the best podiatrist in your community, and it is fine to say that, but do not claim you are the best one in the world—unless the international medical community agrees.

Your branding works best when it feels authentic. It should be strong but not to the point where it would make Will Ferrell jump up and down.

Brand Everywhere

Once you have decided on your brand, make sure it is a part of every part of your business. Here is a partial list where it should be featured:

- Letterhead
- Business Cards
- Invoices/Receipts
- Advertising
- Social Media
- Signatures

- Your Website
- Packaging
- Appointment Cards
- Signage
- Email

In other words, wherever your public encounters something that came from your business, it should feature your branding statement or visual. If you think it is overkill to do that, here is a branding rule of thumb to live by: By the time you are getting sick of your own branding, that is about the time the general public is just *beginning* to notice it and remember it. Keep going!

Before closing this chapter, I want to offer one final piece of proof of the power of branding. Remember when the economy basically drove off a cliff in late 2008 and how hard the recession initially hit us all? According to a Harris Poll, around a third of consumers refused to abandon brand name products for cheaper generic ones, even when their wallets were growing mighty thin.

Brands deliver a big time ROI. Be sure to take the time and make the effort to build one of your own to realize long-lasting success.

In the next chapter, we will drill deeper into helping you do that.

Chapter 10
A Story That Sells

Creating & Maintaining a Memorable Brand Message

A guy walks into a bar with a duck sitting on his head...

Want to know how that comes out? I bet you do. Why? It is the beginning of a story and if there is anything we humans are a sucker for, it is a story. That is why stories are one of the most critical ingredients of a successful brand, as well as effective marketing.

When IBM was first becoming a computer behemoth in the 50's and 60's, they summed up their brand and their story in one work—"Think."

When Apple resurged in the late 90's, they built on the IBM brand story by adding an extra word—"Think *Different.*"

McDonalds once summed up its brand story with the tagline, *"Food, Folks and Fun."* Can you think of anything more fitting than that for their brand?

What is your story? How can you tell it the most effectively? Let me help you find out.

The Power of Storytelling

First, you have to understand why stories are so important. From cave drawings to the Bible to the movies and TV shows of today, humankind has always loved to tell and hear stories. According to recent research, there are big scientific reasons for that. Here are a few discoveries:

- Researchers at the Center for Neuroeconomics Studies at Claremont Graduate University, in Claremont, California discovered that stories activate the oxytocin hormone in our brains, which the scientific community has labeled the love hormone. That is because it is associated with romantic attachment, human bonding, and yes, sex.
- Jeffrey Zacks of Washington University in St. Louis ran brain scans on people reading a story or watching a movie and

64

discovered that, when the main character encountered a situation, it activated the same parts of the brain in the subjects that would have responded if *they themselves* had been in the same predicament in real life. In other words, we heavily identify with stories and feel as though they are happening to us.

- Read Montague of Virginia Tech University in Blacksburg and William Casebeer of the US Defense Advanced Research Projects Agency also analyzed how listening to a story affects the brain, specifically, its reward centers (the parts that respond to such wonderful things as sex, good food and drugs). His conclusion was that certain kinds of stories were actually addictive like a drug and gave the brain a jolt of pleasure.

- Neuroscientist Michael Gazzaniga, from the University of California, Santa Barbara, discovered that we actually use stories to connect things together. It is how we make sense of the world and it is why our ancestors made up stories about gods to explain changes in weather and other natural phenomena. When we cannot explain something, we create a story that will do the job for us, even though the story might be completely wrong.

- Finally, researchers Melanie C. Green and Timothy C. Brock of Ohio State University looked at how stories can impact your belief systems. They found out that "…the reader loses access to some real-world facts in favor of accepting the narrative world that the author has created. While the person is immersed in the story, he or she may be less aware of real-world facts that contradict assertions made in the narrative." To put that in plain English, a *compelling story can be more important to someone than the facts.*

To sum all this up, everybody's brain is conditioned to want stories. We cannot get enough of them, and that brings us to this chapter's ROI Guy Rule:

ROI Guy Rule

A powerful authentic story is the strongest tool you can use to sell yourself, your business and your products.

Now, let us get going and tell your tale.

What Is Your Best Story?

There are several angles you can use to develop your brand story and it will really depend on which one makes for the best story. Here are a few approaches:

Personality-Based Story

If there is something distinctive about you that you can market to make your business more memorable, that is an awesome thing to latch on to. People like to connect with personalities and if you have one that stands out, use it for your brand.

For example, Richard Branson, the head of Virgin, has a personality-based brand story of being an adventurer, a dashing businessman who takes chances and does things differently. Donald Trump, of course, has the image of a straight-talking billionaire who does not take crap from anybody, even if his opinions bring him a host of detractors.

Wherever people like that go, they carry their brand story with them, and more importantly, they stick to their brand story. Trump shows up at an event and says something that makes everybody's hair stand up. Richard Branson will typically show up at a press event in a speedboat with two bikinied models on each arm because he knows that is what people expect from him.

I have a personality-based brand story myself, as "The ROI Guy." That nickname tells potential leads that I am all about my clients' bottom lines and helping them realize more profits from their marketing as well as their office operations. Unfortunately, the bikinied models do not fit in with my brand story, maybe I should rethink it.

Seriously, this is how simple a brand story is, and it is a story. Trump and Branson carry with them a narrative that people define them by. Undoubtedly, the story only applies to the public part of their personalities, but that is the only part that matters in successful marketing.

As noted in an earlier chapter, you can use someone else for a personality-based brand story. You can hire a spokesperson or use someone from your office who has a distinctive (or even an outrageous) persona. Make sure whoever that person is, they are going to be around for a while, so you do not have to start from scratch when they make their exit!

Benefit-Based Story

Robert Kiyosaki wrote a book called *Rich Dad, Poor Dad,* telling the stories of how one dad got rich and another dad stayed poor. His brand story is that he knows how to make you the rich dad and avoid being the failure father. From the book, which articulated his basic brand story, he built a multi-million dollar motivational business, because he has a huge built-in benefit to his brand story, his customers' financial success.

My wife's dental practice, The Sand Lake Centre for Advanced Dentistry (free plug!), is similarly benefit-based. For example, the URL for her website is not the name of the practice, instead it is, BestOrlandoCosmeticDentistry.com. That makes a big statement right there, as does her biography, which is featured on her site. It does not start with where she grew up or where she went to school, it starts with this line: *"Almost every day, Dr. Lisa Peters-Seppala gets to witness the moment when a patient looks in the mirror and finally sees the smile of their dreams."* This is the story that is important to her success, not the facts of her life.

Price/Value-Based Story

You want a simple brand story? Drive by a 99 Cent Store. Their brand story is right there in their name. Similarly, Wal-Mart built their retail empire on the slogan, "Always Low Prices" and more recently, "Save Money. Live Better." Their brand story is all about being able to buy stuff at cheap prices.

Low prices are always an attractive brand story, unless they call the quality of a product or service into serious question. For instance, a discount surgeon may not be the guy you want to work on your internal organs!

Experience-Based Story

All things being equal, one way a brand can make itself stand out is by creating a story where the best possible experience is promised. A few chapters ago, we mentioned Zappos and their commitment to providing the highest levels of customer service. They sold the same shoes as pretty much everyone else but they used their service component to create a compelling story that drew in a whole lot of customers.

A hotel chain like the Ritz-Carlton also has a brand story that is all about customer service, as well as luxurious accommodations. It would be the absolute wrong move for them to promote discount prices since it would contradict their primary brand story.

Completely Made-Up Story

Do you think there are really elves in a tree somewhere making Keebler cookies? Of course not! If there were, they would probably have a reality show on The Food Network!

Seriously, you can sometimes create a fun story to "explain" your product or service, as long as you do not sell anything that is very life-and-death in nature. Cookies and breakfast cereals can have magical creatures in their marketing. Personal injury lawyers, probably not.

Putting Your Story to Work

Whatever your brand story happens to be, you have to take the proper steps to establish it with the public so that it is believable and memorable. If they do not believe your brand story is true, or they simply do not pay attention to it, then it is not going to do you a whole bunch of good. Be sure to keep in mind these marketing do's and don'ts when you are marketing with your brand story.

Do Make Sure to Back Up Your Brand Story!

If my wife, the wonderfully talented dentist (another free plug!), had advertised her practice as the "best Orlando cosmetic dentistry" but did not know how to deliver the services, patients would catch on fast. Similarly, if Richard Branson got seasick when he was riding in on his speedboat with the bikinied models, that would be a blow to his brand story. It is important, especially when you are first marketing your story, to have proof that your story is valid and true. Make sure your business is what you say it is before you get your brand out there, or disaster could result. Have you ever seen how fast social media takes down a lie these days? You do not want to get your own negative Twitter hashtag!

Don't Be Afraid to Blow Your Own Horn When It's Time!

When you have all the pieces put together, or when you know your story is ready for marketing, then be bold and make whatever claim you can, as strongly as you can. There is a lot of competition and if you have developed an effective brand story that gives you an edge over everybody else, use it as much as you can to underline your advantage for anyone considering buying the product or service you are selling.

Do Leverage Every Opportunity!

Look for ways to sell your story every place you can. I will talk a little more about this in the next chapter, but you should make sure your staff is aware of your brand story and knows how to convey it in communications with customers and prospects. I hope I have made it clear, a unified front is important when you are trying to create a unified brand.

Don't Forget to Engage!

Use every opportunity to engage your customers with your brand, so they can actually participate in your branding. You can do this through social media, videos, contests and other interactive marketing techniques that inspire active responses from your audience, rather than having them sold to passively.

Do Continue to Grow and Change!
Marketing greats do not let their brands stand still and you should not either. Times change, your customers change and, no doubt, your business will change as well. If your branding does not continue to evolve with all of these factors, it will be left behind in the dust.

There is a reason Coke, McDonalds, Apple and all the rest change up their branding every couple of years. They want to keep their imagery "fresh," while keeping their main storytelling intact.

Branding can require adjustments for a variety of other reasons as well; for instance, you might spot a weakness in your marketing effectiveness that needs addressing (maybe it is too male-based and you are not reaching enough female customers, or vice-versa).

What is important is to keep tabs on your branding story and how it currently relates to your position in the marketplace. Reflect the present, not the past.

ROI Power Plays: Making Your Storytelling Sizzle

Stay Consistent and Continuous

Once the public has heard and accepted your branding story, you have completed a great, hard-won step. However it is easy to disrupt all that successful branding work if you end up contradicting your own story.

For instance, imagine computer genius Bill Gates not being able to work a Smartphone, or mega-mogul Donald Trump having his credit card declined! In both cases, their brand stories would be short-circuited in a second and they would end up being the subject of a lot of ridicule.

In real life, these kinds of contradictions happen all the time. Keep tight control of your branding to make sure it is consistent and continuous. Not only do those two qualities make sure your brand holds together over the long haul, they also help to reinforce your story to prospects and customers alike.

Stay Simple and Authentic

Ever watch a TV show or movie where the plot gets so complicated you cannot follow it and you finally decide it is more trouble than it is worth? After all, it is supposed to be entertaining, not perplexing.

Likewise, your audience should not have to invest too much brain power following your brand story. Otherwise, they will bolt for a competitor who is more clear-cut. For example, when you put together a website that tells five different stories about eighteen different things you do, it only creates confusion in your prospects' minds. They cannot see any clear reason to buy from you. Your brand story should never get too complicated. It should be a simple narrative people can latch onto quickly and easily recall.

Hold Everyone Accountable to Your Brand Story (Especially Yourself!)

If your brand story is "The Friendliest Place to Shop," and you catch a cashier insulting a customer about his ugly shirt, then guess what? Anyone who witnesses that interaction will not believe your brand story. Likewise, if you are the boss and you chew out an employee in full view of a group of people shopping at your store, those people will very probably tell everyone they know about how the management really acts at the so-called "Friendliest Place to Shop."

It is important that your staff is trained in your brand story and it is even more important that you stay true to it yourself. You may be in charge, but you also have the power to do the most damage to your own business if you disregard your own marketing.

Remember how we started this chapter? "A guy walks into a bar with a duck sitting on his head..."

Stories are effective because we always want to know what happens next (especially if it can benefit us as consumers). Tell your brand story as best as you can and you will attract more than customers; you will attract fans and advocates who appreciate how you do business.

By the way, that guy who walked into a bar with a duck on his head? Here is what happened next. The bartender asks, "Where did you get that thing?" and the duck replies, "I won him in a raffle."

Read on after you are done groaning.

Chapter 11
Put It There, Pal

Creating a Media Placement Strategy

I am going to brag a little here. I have been in videos. I have done audio CDs. I have been in brochures. I have done emails, websites, postcards, mail packages, books and magazines. I have also been on TV and that is not all. Additionally I have done blogs, articles, social media, and speaking engagements. In other words, I have done pretty much everything, except dinner theatre!

I do all this because (a) I love to market and (b) I know it works. More importantly, it helps me to find out what marketing works the best.

This is important simply because, these days, there are a million places to market. You can put your face on bus stop benches or on television monitors in your doctor's office, or on the movie screen before the latest superhero saga unspools. These are only the tip of the iceberg. I believe there must be a secret agency dedicated to finding a thousand or so new places to market to people on a monthly basis. If there happens to be a few inches of space someplace where someone might look, at some point, somebody is going to put an ad there.

I had one client put his phone number on his golf balls because, he figured rightly, he would be losing a few somewhere over the course of the 18 holes. Tiger Woods, he is not, but a marketer he is!

Whenever you finalize the "what" of a campaign (what your message is going to be, what audience you are going to sell to, etc.), your next step is to figure out where best to place your campaign. All the choices can make that step very bewildering so it is best to understand the different kinds of venues where your marketing can appear as well as what their various advantages and disadvantages are. Which, coincidentally, is exactly what I am about to tell you!

Behind the Many Media Channels

Twenty or thirty years ago, this chapter would be a lot shorter since I would be writing about only a few of these channels. As I noted previously, there are a multitude you could be using to promote your business. Some are uniquely positioned to sell your services in an incredibly powerful way; others will not do the job you want them to. You will not know how effective they are for *your* business until you try a few of them out and see what kind of results you get.

The idea, obviously, is to spend "x" amount of dollars on using a particular media channel and get "y" amount of dollars back in sales. Naturally, you want "y" to be a lot bigger than "x." The good news is, for many of these media channels, your initial investment is not going to be all that costly.

The other good news is that the technology is readily available to monitor how many leads a campaign generates, as well as how much profit each marketing placement generates for you.

The next section will be devoted to that technology and I will share a few case studies that will make your eyes pop. For now, I just want you to know that systems are available so you can determine, down to the penny, how much money a single marketing placement makes for your business.

Undoubtedly, you are using some of the channels I am about to mention but chances are you have not used them all. Hopefully, this chapter will motivate you to think beyond your current marketing box of tricks and check out some of the other ones you have either been ignoring or telling yourself they would not work for you.

Keep in mind this chapter's big rule:

ROI GUY RULE
If you put a dollar towards a marketing campaign—you should expect to get more than that dollar back!

Advertising is designed to make you money. It does not matter if you or your spouse, or your assistant, or the guy who mows your lawn really, really likes a marketing campaign you are doing; if it is not making you money or if it is not making sales, why are you bothering? Does the opinion of the guy who mows your lawn really matter more than generating revenue?

Of course, there are some cases where you market with a different purpose other than immediate profits in mind, such as building your brand, raising your profile or demonstrating your expertise. Those all have their own value, as I have discussed before. However, if you are marketing to build your bankroll, then leave yours and everyone else's opinion out of it. It does not matter what you or someone else likes, it matters what causes a prospect buy from you. Business is business and if you do not focus your marketing on boosting your bottom line, you are flushing money down the toilet. Was that too graphic? Okay, you are throwing money out the window.

On the other hand, maybe you are not spending enough money. Maybe the cost of some of the channels I am going to talk about has put you off, especially if you are a smaller business. I can understand that, being a bit of a one-man band myself.

From personal experience, I can also tell you, that the more you experiment with different channels and different campaigns, the more sophisticated (and profitable) your marketing will become, if you put the systems in place to accurately measure the success of each campaign (and again, I will talk about those systems in the next section).

Remember, once you determine what works, your marketing will not be costing you anything. As a matter of fact, it will be doing what it is supposed to be doing, making you money. Not only that, you will stop losing money on marketing that does not work. Sure, the guy who mows your lawn might be upset that your commercial is no longer playing at 5:00 a.m. on the local sports network but, since that commercial only brought you $3 worth of business, give him a nice tip at Christmas and he will weather the storm.

All I am saying is give these channels a chance. Initially, it may seem like your cash flow is taking a big hit by paying for these campaigns but that money comes back to you big-time when you hit on your most effective strategies. You end up making more money, picking up more new customers, and making more sales. That is how a business grows!

The Top Media Channels

For the purposes of this chapter, I am going to break down the media channels into nine main categories. Obviously, you can list a million different ways to market but, in my humble opinion, these are the best umbrella groups to classify them under.

Print

Magazines and newspapers are increasingly being seen as dinosaurs (and you know what happened to them). Yes, they are part of the traditional old media but they still can be very effective. It is a good place to reach older demographics, as well as smarter and richer demographics. More importantly, a print advertisement is easily torn out of the periodical and saved. That makes it easy for someone who is interested in the ad to have all your information without having to worry about memorizing your name, phone number or website URL.

Another way to use print is to actually get a story done about you in the local publication. This is much easier to accomplish with small local periodicals, like a weekly paper with a limited distribution because they are often begging for articles to print. The size of the paper does not matter much, if it has quality readership in an affluent section of town that you want to reach. The fact that you are a featured story gives you a big boost of credibility and builds your brand.

When it comes to print, do not forget other traditional marketing tools such as the Yellow Pages. Many businesses are dropping out of these kinds of publications, leaving the field wide open to the businesses that not only stay in them, but actually buy more space so they can fully dominate their business sector. I have clients that swear by them and, since they use my marketing tracking systems to determine their ads' ROI, I believe them!

Public Relations

Public relations, is another old media favorite that has plenty of new media applications. If you want to promote a new hire, a new location or a new product or service, it has never been easier (or more affordable) to create and submit press releases to various online publications and websites. Not only that, but the more you do it, the higher you rank on Google search results.

Depending on the size and scope of your business, media kits distributed to local and national media can also prime the pump for interviews and stories based on your particular expertise. In general, this tactic is more of an image-builder than a sale, but, used correctly, it can create the kind of credibility you need to boost your sales conversions and help you reach audiences you might not reach with conventional advertising.

Seminars & Speaking Engagements

If you are a business-to-business operation or selling to a very specific audience base (such as real estate investors), seminars and speaking engagements are a great way to promote who you are and what you do. In-person marketing opportunities give you a chance to put a face on your business and make a strong personal connection.

These kinds of events also give you the time and the platform to sell your product or service at the end of your talk, immediately after your audience has been exposed to your ideas for a nonstop hour (or however long your presentation is).

If you have a good personality for public speaking, you will find this to be a very effective media channel to connect with prospects.

Direct Mail

Here we go again, another marketing technique most people believe is passé. Snail mail? Seriously? Wait for longer than two seconds for something to get somewhere? What is this, the Stone Age?

And yet...

Remember when you could not throw out "junk mail" fast enough because it constantly filled up your mailbox? Guess what? Now there is practically nothing else to compete for a postal customer's attention because so much marketing is done virtually! With the vast majority of marketing being done through emails and other online strategies, a direct mail piece is no longer junk, but a fascinating rarity that recipients will actually look at and read. Wow.

It is the same principle as the Yellow Pages. If you make a splash in a place where all the competition has left the building, you become the big fish. In the case of physical mail, everyone still gets it, why not use it? An attention-getting mailing, with an inexpensive "free" gift or an effective headline on the outside, can generate a lot of interest and a lot of sales. Do not write off snail mail just yet.

Direct mail can also be targeted to your ideal customer much more easily and precisely. This is another concept I will discuss in detail in the next section of this book. Rest assured if you only want to reach blue-eyed Eskimos who drive KIAs and shop at Home Depot, we can make it happen!

A final note, many businesses send out monthly newsletters. Research shows, pretty conclusively, that if you send yours through the mail, there is a much better chance it will be read than if you had simply sent it through in email form. People are pretty fast on the trigger with their "Delete" buttons these days!!!

Video

Whether you are placing a TV commercial on a local station or posting a video on YouTube, video is one of the most effective media channels available. You are able to rehearse and edit your presentation until it is polished to the max, then record it for posterity. Not only that, but, by putting yourself on camera, you can make that all-important personal connection, without actually having to go anywhere!

Online video is also great if you need a lot of time to explain your product or service. Sometimes people want more detailed information about your process or how you deliver what you say you are going to deliver. Producing a straightforward video about what you do and posting it on social media and your website home page (you will find one on mine at www.TheROIMatrix.com) is an easy way to communicate directly with leads who may not yet be motivated enough to call and ask for more details.

Audio

Who needs pictures? An audio information product can also pay off big for a business. People spend a lot of time in their cars and walking their dogs listening to podcasts and CDs and you almost always have their full attention while they do it. Producing informative audio products can help you sell your business and your services while educating the listener.

Online Marketing

Blogs. Landing pages. Email campaigns. Pay-Per-Click ads. Content marketing. Membership sites. SEO and SEM. You could fill about a million books like this one with all the different ways you can use the internet to sell your stuff, therefore, I am not going to attempt to explain it all in a few paragraphs here (although I will talk about it in the next section of the book). The thing to remember is that most consumers now make their buying choices *online;* therefore, you want to have as strong a presence as possible. The best online marketing strategy depends on what your business is all about and who your desired customers are. The good news is, as with off-line marketing, you can easily target your campaigns and track the effectiveness of them to see which are making the most sales for you.

Social Media

It is vital to have your own professional website, but you have to realize that most people are not going to make more than one or two visits to it. When you want to sell your stuff, you need to go to where the people are and these days: they are on Facebook, Twitter, LinkedIn, Pinterest and other social media sites.

When you tap into the crowds that are buzzing around social media services, you have the ability to create your own following and then drive them back to your site. Remember to post interesting, entertaining or informative content that pertains to what you do. People are not going to be interested in pictures of your lunch (at least I am not because I would rather eat food than look at it). I will have more on social media in the chapter after next.

Points of Contact

Most businesses have what I call "points of contacts" with the public that provide marketing opportunities. I am talking about things like:

- Appointment cards
- Email signatures
- Promotional giveaways
- Business cards
- Letterhead
- Employees

These points of contact are usually professional and boring, because they are not seen as anything but providing a function. Part of their function can be marketing. Do not be shy about putting your primary marketing message front and center on some of these points of contact because they can be invaluable to your branding efforts

Yes, the last item on that list was, in fact, "employees". Your staff, if you have one, is often your main representative to the general public, and they should always be aware of your marketing aims from personal experience.

ROI Power Plays: Charging Up Your Media Channel Strategy

Don't Rely on Anecdotal Evidence!
Your aunt, at a family gathering, comes up to you and tells you how much she loves, L-O-V-E-S, your billboard on the highway. "Wow," you think to yourself, "that billboard is worth the thousands of dollars I spent on it!"

Every time you review your marketing budget, however, the huge expense of that billboard sticks out like a sore thumb. Then you think of your aunt's glowing endorsement of it and you keep renewing the contract, even though it may not be bringing in any revenue.

With apologies to all your relatives out there, anecdotal evidence—something someone happens to say to you—is the *wrong* way to evaluate your marketing campaigns' effectiveness. Your aunt, or anyone who knows you or uses your business, will naturally notice a marketing placement and mention it to you. This does not mean, however, that campaign works for the average consumer who does not know you. That is why marketing tracking is vital to evaluating cost verses revenue of each piece of advertising.

Understand Your Strategy Before Choosing Channels
Think about what you are trying to accomplish before you choose which media channel to use for your next campaign. For example, if you need to explain or demonstrate a product or procedure, YouTube videos, promoted through social media, may be your best bet. If you are hard-selling a big discount or sale, direct mail coupons or an email campaign might be the way to go.

Every campaign has different needs and every channel has different advantages. Mix and match for marketing success!

Fill in the Gaps by Targeting Groups

You may be using one-size-fits-all marketing and missing out on specific groups that would buy from you if they only knew what you were offering. For example, a dentist may be promoting dental implants, but not effectively reaching seniors, their biggest market for that product. In that case, he or she might consider going out and speaking to senior groups directly to make that important one-on-one connection while helping them understand the very real benefits of dental implants to older people (did I mention my wife's a dentist?).

Look for ways to use your media channels to target specific niche groups that would most likely buy a certain product or service.

Again, you never know what works until you try it and track it. Be creative, but be practical, when making your media placement plans.

Want to know what the follow-up to this chapter is going to be? Follow-up marketing! Funny how that works.

Chapter 12
Don't Stop Until They Get Enough

Why Follow-Up Marketing Is Crucial!

Well, you tried.

I mean, right? You gave it your best shot. You presented the best case to a potential customer for why they should buy from you.

And they said, "No."

Fine. Move on with your life. Plenty of fish (with money) in the sea. Go on and sell to somebody else, right?

As you might be able to tell from the title of this particular chapter, *wrong*. Follow-up marketing should be an *essential* component of anyone's sales systems and you are about to find out why it is so important to your ongoing ROI.

Once is Not Enough

One sales attempt almost *never* does the trick. People have to be comfortable with you, trust you and feel okay about giving you money (unless it's a very minor purchase).

That does not happen with one marketing attempt. If you do not believe me, maybe you will believe these statistics from National Sales Executive Association:

- 2% of sales are made on the first contact
- 3% of sales are made on the second contact
- 5% of sales are made on the third contact
- 10% of sales are made on the fourth contact
- 80% of sales are made on the fifth to twelfth contact

See what I mean? 80% of the time, it takes five or more times to close the deal and yet many businesspeople are unaware of this fact of life. Check out these statistics from the same study:

- 48% of salespeople *never* follow up with a prospect

- 25% of salespeople make a second contact and stop
- 12% of salespeople only make three contacts and stop
- Only 10% of salespeople make more than three contacts

That is right, 90% of salespeople quit before they have their best shot at a new customer.

In marketing circles, every time you make contact with a lead or a customer in order to make a sale is called a "touch." The above statistics make it clear you need to do multiple touches in order to trigger a sale.

Why does it take a consumer so long to actually buy or accept the product or service, even after they understand what is being offered? There are two important factors that contribute to a sale: *trust* and *relationships.*

Think of the first attempt at a sale as a first date. Then think about how horrible a first date can be. You do not feel you can totally trust the other person because you do not really know them yet. It takes a few dates to discover if there is a possibility of a future relationship and if you actually like and trust them.

Most people are equally reluctant to part with what is in their wallets as what is in their hearts. They do not want to let a business get to third base, let alone make it to home plate, until they are sure that business is the one for them.

You need to go beyond thinking about how to meet a customer's needs and begin to think about how you can make the customer *trust* you to meet those needs.

Be There When They Are Ready

Building trust begins before they are even ready to buy. What do people do when they are considering something bigger than groceries or gas? They do research, probably online. They check out who has the best price, who has the best service, etc. They are basically in search of free information that will help them make the right choice and that is your golden opportunity to have your "first date" with this particular lead.

When your website offers a free special report, eBook, or access to an instructional video—in exchange for the lead's name and email address— you now have what you need to begin your sales relationship with them. To continue the dating analogy, think of it as getting a phone number from someone in a bar who might be interested in you.

As the lead continues to think about choices of whom to buy from, you continue "dating" them. You send a series of mostly informational emails about what they are interested in. Do not be pushy, nobody likes an aggressive date. Instead, be nice and helpful and provide facts they can use, rather than hype.

Focus on the benefits of the product or service, so they understand what they will get out of it. Maybe drop in a comparison about what you do and what your competition does not do.

As you continue to communicate, you might want to provide "touchstones of trust". For example, testimonials from some of your satisfied customers, or third party articles about your business which are obviously favorable.

Why are you doing all this before the lead is ready to actually buy? Here is another important statistic, courtesy of the Harvard Business Review: 60% of people, when they are finally ready to make the purchase, *already know who they are going to buy from.* No, they are not psychic. It is because they are buying from someone they have already have bought from in the past or *someone they already know.*

Remember, I said 80% of sales are made after the fourth "touch." You have already put in your time, if you have made contact with that person three or four times before they are ready to buy.

You have a much better chance of getting that sale if you have established: (a) who you are (b) your expertise in the product or service category and (c) your trustworthiness.

Also remember, even if they buy from somebody else instead of you, they have already established their interest in what you sell. They may have a bad experience with that other business or they may see how your business could have brought them a better benefit with their purchase.

That is why you never give up on them, which finally brings us to this chapter's ROI Guy Rule (better late than never!):

ROI Guy Rule

NEVER lose a lead!

Hang onto them until they "buy or die!"

Yes, "buy or die" sounds harsh but I am not talking about anything involving funerals. What I am saying is you want to keep marketing to your leads until they either become a paying customer or you are no longer able to market to them (they unsubscribe from your emails, they move, their email address stops working, etc.). If you do not do this then you are leaving money on the table.

All of this sounds like an ongoing pain-in-the-neck that will have you spending all your waking hours marketing to these people instead of attending to your core business. The good news is, as you will see in the final section of this book, there are amazing ways to automate the entire follow-up process.

When you put those systems in place, you and your staff literally never have to lift a finger to make that continuous marketing happen because it is all done with "computer-internety" type of stuff. Is this not specific enough? Do not worry; a little later, I will throw around enough big words to make your head spin. The important thing to know is that automated follow-up marketing is the only foolproof way to make sure you keep all your leads in your marketing loop. If you have a business, you should appreciate anything that makes you money without you having to do anything!

After the Sale: Why Stop Now?

The difficult part of marketing is getting a *new* customer. Now that you have cleared that high hurdle, you have the person's complete contact information and their trust (provided you have sold them a product they love as well as provided great pro-active customer service).

Once someone has bought from you and felt good about the experience, they are very likely to buy from you again. That is why you keep your buyer relationship going with them *after* you have made the sale.

Too many businesses only focus on getting new customers. Various studies show that it costs anywhere from five to seven times as much money to get a new customer, as it is to sell something to an existing one. Yes, you need to keep attracting new buyers to keep your business growing and thriving but do not forget to look in your own backyard. There is plenty of gold to dig for in your existing customer list.

This is a lesson that big profitable mega-businesses like Amazon learned early on. If you frequently buy from the virtual warehouse that is Amazon, you are aware that, every time you log onto the site, it immediately suggests products that are related in some way to your prior purchases. Darned if it does not work. At some point, I will have to disable that one-click shopping option before I go broke!

Netflix does the same kind of thing. Its streaming service is famous for suggesting other movies and TV shows that are the like the ones you have already watched. Why does that matter, if you are paying a flat monthly fee for the streaming? They do it because they never want you to think they are out of things that you might want to watch and, therefore, stop paying the flat fee. That points out another good reason to keep marketing to your current customers; you do not want them to wander away to a competitor.

There is no reason not to do follow-up marketing and every reason to engage in it. Let us look at a few ROI Power Plays to make yours all that it can be.

ROI Power Plays: Firing Up Your Follow-Up Marketing

Continue to Communicate with Auto-responders

Auto-responders, when used for marketing purposes, are a sequence of prewritten emails (hopefully personalized by whatever marketing software you use) that are sent out at programmed intervals (one every couple of days or once a week or monthly, whatever works best for what you are trying to accomplish).

Auto-responders are usually designed to either: (a) educate your customers and leads (and subtly sell your services) or (b) promote a special sale or discounted item, whatever the case may be, make sure that your auto-responders are provided with some kind of unique value. In other words, you do not want to clog up someone's email inbox without a good reason.

For instance, a dentist might send out a series of auto-responders written to educate his or her patients about their sedation dentistry options. Here is an example of one that my wife's practice actually uses:

SUBJECT HEADING: Why You're Not Alone in Fearing the Dentist

Hi {FIRST NAME}, I wanted to tell you that if you are experiencing fear about dental visits and that fear is preventing you from obtaining needed dental care, you are far from alone.

Studies show that nearly 30% of ALL Americans are afraid of the dentist and avoid dental care at all costs.

Our practice spends a lot of time trying to reach people who may be suffering from this fear, because we know how dangerous it can be to put off treatment that's critical to both their appearance and their overall health.

The truth is that dentistry does not have to be painful or scary, because we've developed special ways to relax patients and put them completely at ease. Through Oral Sedation Dentistry, we've successfully treated many people who never thought they could get through a dental appointment.

Most people don't know about Sedation Dentistry, or the fact that it makes any dental treatment as painless as possible. You are given a small pill to take about an hour before your dental appointment. A friend or family member should accompany you to our offices, because you will feel a little drowsy. No needles are necessary.

One of our expert team members will monitor you and your vital signs at all times when you are in our chair, while we take care of your dental needs. When treatment is completed, your companion will take you home for a comfortable rest.

Our goal is to keep you comfortable and for you to have the best possible experience, with very little pain and anxiety, so you can look better now and feel better in the long run.

I would love to personally discuss the options we can give you (or someone you love) to help you get the dental care you require to live a happy, full and healthy life with the attractive, confident, healthy smile you deserve.

Since we offer a very limited number of free consultations, I invite you to call our staff, at your earliest convenience, to discuss your personal situation. Our phone number is _____. There is no obligation, so please don't stress about coming in to see us.

Keep smiling,

(DENTIST NAME) (PRACTICE NAME)

You see how this auto-responder, which is triggered to be sent out after a patient has already indicated interest in pain-free dental treatments, blends facts with benefits? It also uses a friendly, conversational tone. Do the same with yours. Auto-responders are a cheap, easy and effective way to do follow-up marketing and can make a big difference in bringing additional sales to your business.

Create Automatic Follow-up Marketing Sequences

While auto-responders are an effective tool, the most effective follow-up marketing is done via a series of various kinds of "touches."

For example, if someone visits your website and does what we discussed earlier, they leave an email address and name in order to have a free Special Report sent to them, the follow-up sequence might go like this:

Step 1:   Send Free Report #1

Step 2:   Send Email Auto-responder #1

Step 3:   Send Email Auto-responder #2

Step 4:   Send Email Auto-responder #3

Step 5:   Send a Link to a Free Video

Step 6:   Send Email Auto-responder #4

Step 7:   Send Email Auto-responder #5

Step 8:   Send Postcard #1 (I can help my clients get the physical address of a lead through their email address so direct mail becomes an option for them)

Step 9:   Send Email Auto-responder #6

Step 10: Send Postcard #2

Step 11: Send Email Auto-responder #7

Step 12: Send Email Auto-responder #8

Step 13: Send Postcard #3
Step 14: Send Email Auto-responder #9
Step 15: Send Free Report #2 with Offer

This is a very low-cost sequence, with a good mix of hard information and marketing. You might even want to mix a phone call or two in there, if you have the staff to handle it.

Follow-up When They Don't Show

Sometimes, someone says they are going to call and make an appointment to come in to your business (especially if you are a medical or legal practice) and never does. Or worse, they make the appointment and simply do not show up.

Many businesses might call up once to see if the person is going to come in and let it go at that. You should not. Plan a follow-up sequence of postcards and calls, with reasonable intervals between them, to remind the no-shows that they were ready to come in to see you. You might even want to give them an incentive to come back in. If it is the kind of appointment that is easy for them to forget about (in other words, not an emergency or anything urgent), they will, unless you remind them!)

In the final chapter of this section of the book, get ready to face the facts about Facebook and other social media sites as we take an in-depth look at how to realize the greatest ROI from your status updates!

Chapter 13
Improve Your Status

Leveraging Social Media to the Max

You know the Super Bowl? I figured you had probably heard of it. It is easily the biggest sports event of the year. There is a huge audience and well worth the price of admission, right? That depends on your viewpoint. For example, what would you say if I told you there was a way to spend virtually *nothing* and have access to an audience *ten times the size of the audience of the Super Bowl?*

You might say I am crazy, I get that a lot, but I am not exaggerating. When you use social media, you have the potential to connect with the billion-plus people all over the world who use it every day. Therefore, why would you not use it? As a friend of mine likes to say, "You'd be crazy not to."

Now getting back to the Super Bowl.... It is because the Super Bowl draws such a huge audience, that advertisers scramble to get their spots on during the biggest television event of the year. One company paid a record five million dollars for one thirty second commercial in 2013 (a mere $167,000 per second, pocket change, right?). Why would they put up that kind of money? The answer is simple; they are able to deliver their message directly to over 100 million people who are watching the football game. That leads us to this chapter's rule:

ROI Guy Rule

Social Media is where the people are, so—

it's where YOU need to be too!

The Revolution is Not Over!

Before I talk specifically about social media, you first have to understand that we have just been through the start of one of the most incredible revolutions in human history.

The Internet has changed everything in a way very few saw coming. Who could have foreseen having all the knowledge we currently have at our disposal? All the music, movies, TV shows and millions of books that are mere keystrokes or button-pushes away.

It does not stop there since social media offers us the most awesome *communication platforms* ever available. When you do it right, you can instantly and effectively communicate with an incredible number of past, present and potentially future customers. This has never been possible before. The closest thing we used to have to it was a "fax blast." You remember, you would send the same fax to a whole bunch of people at the same time (and run up a pretty good phone bill in the process). What fun it was to deal with all that curled paper!

We are in a miraculous age, but miracles become old news fast and already many people are starting to think of social media as being as exciting as a gramophone. However, the fact is the revolution is far from over. It is still going on and you should definitely be on the front lines.

The Fast and Furious Growth of Social Media

How do I know the social media revolution is still happening? Way back in the dark ages, (i.e. 2002), Friendster.com started it all. Since then, it has continued its onward march to MySpace, YouTube, Facebook, Twitter, Google+, and, most recently, Pinterest, which caught fire in 2011. Who knows what will be next? It is pretty clear that social media is here to stay and that it has become a part of almost everyone's everyday lives. 67% of online adults use Facebook while 40% of cell phone users visit a social network site on their mobile device.

Big business players understand those numbers, which is why three-fourths of all Fortune 500 companies have corporate Twitter accounts and two-thirds of them have a Facebook page. A new survey shows that, by 2015, over *eight billion dollars* will be spent on marketing through social media, with companies devoting about 19% of their marketing budgets in the virtual arena.

A few more significant statistics:

- Around *60 percent* of B2B marketers found improved search rankings from their social media outreach

- An incredible *77 percent* of B2C companies and 43 percent of B2B companies acquire customers from Facebook

- An overwhelming *90 percent* of consumers use online information to decide on who they are going to buy from.

- Social media has a *100 percent* higher lead-to-close rate than outbound marketing.

Social media is not just about re-tweeting jokes or posting pictures of your lunch. It is about marketing and selling. To accomplish these two important business goals, you have to find ways of engaging with your audience. Gone are the days where you can have a brochure website or a static social media profile page with no ongoing activity. You need a constant and consistent social media strategy.

Of course, with all the choices out there, choices that are constantly changing, it is easy to get confused about what your strategy should be. In this chapter, I am going to give you some general tips to help you devise your strategy. Of course, you will have to do some research on your own to see what will be the most powerful and integrated social media solution for your specific business. Different sites work better for different niches. The best thing to do is check on what your biggest competitors are doing. See where they are succeeding on social media and how you can make your own mark on the same sites.

In the meantime, here are a few ingredients you should always add to your social media stew:

Always provide value

Have you ever had a Facebook friend who used their statuses to relentlessly promote their own business? Or defriended someone who was annoying because they never provided anything interesting or fun? I have been tempted and my whole business is marketing!

Nobody likes nonstop advertising that offers nothing but hype and hard sell tactics. That is why the most important aspect of your social media strategy should be to always provide value. That value can be in the form of useful facts or advice that relates to your specialty, discounts or special offers every so often, or links to informative articles or videos (especially if they are created by you!). I will talk a little more about how to create fun and engaging interaction a little later.

Carve out regular time for social media

If you think you do not have time to tweet or update your Facebook status or post on whatever your preferred social media sites happen to be, I am willing to bet you are wrong. Not a lot of money, mind you, but maybe a couple of nickels. The truth is social media does not demand a huge amount of time from you in order for you to create an effective presence.

As a matter of fact, you could devote as little as fifteen minutes a day, or even every other day, and make it work for you. The important thing is to develop the habit of social media in order that it becomes a fixed and scheduled task. Unless that habit is in place, you will not have a shot at building the following you want to have. If you really do not have the time, assign the task to a staffer who is savvy about social media (with direction from you, of course!).

Do not assume your audience is not using social media.
Some still believe that social media is only being used by kids, teens and "twenty-somethings". Nothing could be further from the truth. As a matter of fact, the fastest-growing demographic in social media these days is seniors, even though, in fact, every conceivable age group is embracing social media sites. Whoever you are targeting, they are on social media somewhere.

Do not try to attract everybody or be everywhere.
While people like Ashton Kutcher may have over fourteen million Twitter followers, but as much as I hate to have to say this, you are not Ashton Kutcher. You do not need millions; you may not even need hundreds of followers. What you want is quality, not quantity, when it comes to your social media troops. You want people who are interested in the kind of product or service you deliver and might be inclined to buy from you. When your social media strategy is targeted correctly, that is exactly the kind of people you will pick up.

Similarly, because there are so many social media sites, you might feel intimidated and say to yourself, "I can't post on all of these sites, I just can't do this!" You are right. You cannot do that, unless it is your full-time job, but you do not have to. You simply have to choose two or three sites that work best for your kind of business.

Remember a couple of chapters ago when we talked about all the media channels that exist, such as direct mail, video and audio? You do not stop yourself from marketing because there are so many media channels and you should not stop yourself from doing social media because there are so many sites to choose from. It is kind of like not hitting the buffet at a Las Vegas casino because there are too many delicious dishes to choose!

Some businesses are born to interact on LinkedIn, others are perfect for Pinterest and, for still others, Facebook is the best bet. Think about consulting with a social media expert and try to hone in on the site where you will find the most potential customers and get started there!

Also keep in mind that there are applications that allow you to update your status across multiple social media sites and that makes social media multi-tasking a whole lot easier.

Track your results

As I will discuss in the next and final section of this book, when you use online and phone tracking technology, you can instantly find out how many sales are coming from which social media placement. This allows you to create the perfect targeting strategy, because you can see where you make the most sales conversions and where you make the biggest sales in terms of dollars.

Create Interaction

Finally, there are a lot of fun ways you can interact with the public and grow your crowd. For example, one marketer I know holds a "Caption of the Day" contest weekdays on Facebook. He posts a wacky photo of something weird—like a car sitting in a swimming pool—and invites his followers to come up with a funny caption for the situation.

You can also create conversations about your business, such as inviting people to answer trivia questions about your field or asking for others' experiences with your type or product or service, anything that might motivate someone to comment or share your post.

Also, when it comes to content, you do not have to feature only your own. You can find others' reputable online articles, blogs or videos and link to them as well. This not only provides your crowd with new content, it also gives you access to the audience of the authors of the additional content. For example, if you link to a Richard Branson video, those who love Richard Branson will want to check it out.

There are about a million different ways to mix it up, keep it fresh and grow your followers. Try different things and see which ones work the best and then continue to focus and refine your strategy from there.

ROI Power Plays: Creating Super Strong Social Media

Picture It with Pinterest

Many marketers have been slow to take advantage of the sudden surge of popularity of the latest online sensation but the research numbers are too dramatic to ignore. In 2012, Pinterest usage grew by over 1000%. Make no mistake, Facebook is still the social media champ by a huge margin, but Pinterest's marketing firepower is nothing to sneeze at. According to a recent study, fifty brands who did a Pinterest promotion found that it caused a *150%* jump in followers.

Maximize Mobile

NBC News found that the number of people who use the mobile phone and tablet Facebook apps jumped 24% from June to September of 2012, and is now well over 30 million. Facebook understands where the future is. Here is what they had to say about it: *"…we anticipate that the rate of growth in mobile usage will exceed the growth in usage through personal computers for the foreseeable future and that the usage through personal computers may be flat or continue to decline in certain markets."*

Mobile social media marketing requires a slightly different approach that respects consumers who are on the go and, at the same time, creates a positive engagement with them; shift your strategy for mobile if necessary.

Transform Your Customers into Your Salespeople

Who do people trust the most, when it comes to recommendations for products and services? People they know. 92% of consumers listen to friends, family members and co-workers in their circle when they are shopping for something specific. That means the more "fans" and "followers" you attract through your social media efforts, the more "likes" you will motivate and the more "shares" you will inspire, and the more success you will continue to experience.

Social media is now a fact of life, just like movies, TV, radio and other types of media became after they were introduced. That means it can be easy to take it for granted or ignore it altogether, because it has been around a few years. As I hope I have made clear in this chapter this is a mistake. Social media will continue to expand and evolve at a rapid pace and in unexpected ways. Its fast-moving force will provide plenty of potential pay-offs as well. Do not dismiss it because there is simply too much opportunity to develop real connections that pay off in ways that other marketing avenues cannot deliver.

Get ready for the fourth and final section of our book, where I will take you to a level of marketing you probably did not even know existed! You are about to discover technology that can almost guarantee you prospects that will buy—stay tuned!

Section 4
Automating Your ROI Power

This section is where it all comes together. It details how you can use data in exciting new ways that you may never have thought possible.

So far, I have talked about basic principles, strategies and techniques of improving your ROI in every aspect of your business. I have covered marketing basics such as branding, upselling, sales funnels, informational products, social media and follow-up marketing.

Now, I am going to reveal how the right technology can enable you to, in effect, "Super-Size" all those marketing principles in order to create results that were unthinkable a decade or so ago.

In case you are thinking I am making all this stuff up, I am also going to share a few case studies in this section from some of my favorite clients, who have very kindly offered to explain how ROI technology has paid off for their businesses.

Watch out because the ROI Power is about to explode!

Chapter 14
ROI Power Case Study One

Dr. Kelly Brown, Owner of Custom Dental

To begin this section, I thought I would share my first case study to give you an idea of what ROI technology did for Dr. Kelly Brown. Dr. Brown owns ten dental practices, nine in Oklahoma and one in Missouri. With that many offices to look after, our automated ROI technology definitely helps him keep on top of things. Here is Dr. Brown to tell you how:

We began working with Richard close to four or five years ago when his main service was tracking and recording inbound phone calls to our offices. We could evaluate which ads were bringing in the most patients and get an idea of how many leads each piece of marketing was generating so we would know which was the most effective.

> *"It is not guessing,*
>
> *it is not emotional,*
>
> *it is not hearsay,*
>
> *it is <u>factual</u>."*

To this day, we continue to gain a lot of value from the call-tracking system. For example, if we notice a certain office is beginning to slump in terms of converting inquiries into actual appointments. For instance, they get 26 calls from potential patients and only 11 end up going in for an appointment; we listen to those inbound calls so we discover the reason why the closing rate has dropped significantly.

Typically, it is because the person we have answering the phones at that particular office is inept. When that happens, we gather their bad phone call recordings, put them together with some good calls that converted and send them to a trainer. The trainer will personally work with that person by going through what they are doing wrong and help them to do it right.

Last year, we began working with Richard's new system, The ROI Matrix, which he made to interface with our Dentrix dental practice management software. This means when we put in appointments and

93

treatment information about our patients in Dentrix, the data immediately transfers to the Matrix. That software bridge means we can now know how many leads a marketing campaign generates and also how much actual *revenue*. After we log in the cost of each campaign, the Matrix calculates the precise ROI (return on investment) for those individual ads or campaigns. We have the Matrix working at two of our ten practices at the moment, and we hope to have the software bridge up and running for the other eight by the end of the month.

Every day I screen the ROI Matrix and call tracking reports to make sure the ship's heading in the right direction. Just like I pick up the newspaper every morning, I check those reports to see how many calls our ad sources are generating. I basically look at the various categories and numbers for each practice, run the averages of all of them and give them a bubble summary of what is going on and what we can improve, if need be.

For example, if I have one dentist and his average treatment plan costs $1200, and the average for our other doctors is $2800, I know the situation has to be managed. You have to say, "Okay, what's wrong here? Do you need some training in appliances or cosmetic dentistry, or other higher-end options you can offer to your patients?"

I feel what the whole package has given me an accurate decision-making process. I know exactly how much I should pay to get a patient since it is pretty easy to calculate from the ROI metrics and I know whether I should continue to invest in a particular marketing source, or eliminate it because it is not working. I have a way to totally measure my marketing effectiveness because it is not guessing, it is not emotional, and it is not hearsay, it is *factual*.

Now, I cannot say how much I am saving on marketing by doing all this because I have no idea how much I was losing in the past! However, I definitely know it has had a big impact and, of course, it saves me a TON of time.

For example, before I had the ROI Matrix, it took close to fifteen days to get all the reports I required to be done at the end of the month. That is because I was asking my office staff to check out certain patients, gather certain numbers, request certain information, and juggle all that with their regular duties. It is not 15 days of solid work, but 15 days of starting, stopping and waiting for necessary information, then getting it finalized in the ten practices and finally running the averages on all of them.

Last month, at the offices with the ROI Matrix up and running, it was completed in two!

Chapter 15
Your Ideal Customer

Delivering the Most from Your Database

Here is a fun fact you probably did not know: People who watch ABC buy 16% more facial tissues than the average person, whereas people who watch Fox, buy 4% *less* facial tissues. Why? Who knows? Maybe ABC shows make people cry more often, or give them more colds? By the way, we also know that people who watch TV showings of the movie *Braveheart* eat a lot of Pop-Tarts. No lie! Again, why would that be? When Mel Gibson paints his face half-blue, does it make people want a blueberry Pop-Tart? Hmmm....

Here is the great thing about these kinds of weird facts: we do not have to know why. We can argue about it until the cows come home, but it does not really matter. What *does* matter is that a big advertiser like, say, Kleenex, knows where they should put their commercials to reach the most tissue users.

This is something they could not have known until just a few years ago. Big Data, as it is called, enables advertisers to know a lot of things about consumers. This, in turn, helps them achieve a much higher ROI on their marketing because they are able to put their message in front of the kinds of people who are most receptive to them.

Forbes Magazine has called Big Data "the biggest game-changing opportunity for marketing and sales since the Internet went main-stream almost 20 years ago." In the same article, a study of 250 different marketing campaigns showed that when these campaigns were based on data, they showed an ROI that was 15 to 20% higher than normal.[1]

[1]Jonathan Gordon, "Big Data, Analytics and the Future of Marketing and Sales," Forbes, July 22, 2013

In other words, Big Data is BIG!

I have good news for you! I would not be writing this chapter if this marketing miracle could not be delivered to your doorstep. The reason it is so easy for you to use this awesome technique in your business is because all the data you need to start with is already sitting in your business files!

Which leads us to this chapter's ROI Guy Rule:

ROI Guy Rule

Your database is your goldmine and the sooner you start mining, the higher your ROI soars!

The 80/20 Rule

The first part of this chapter's ROI Guy Rule is a pretty common marketing truism. Every marketing expert in the world will tell you that your database is a goldmine. However, the reality was before we learned how to *use* that data; the statement was more bull than bullion.

Certainly, you should be using your database to market aggressively to your list of past and present customers in order to: (a) offer additional products or services (b) upsell them on current ones or (c) get them back in to buy if they have been away. Obviously, as I have discussed earlier in this book, it is important to keep marketing to your current customers. After all, they have already bought from you and hopefully a positive relationship has been established.

Most importantly, you need to keep your top customers in place in order to maintain a consistent cash flow. Top customers are critical to the viability of your business and they usually generate around 80% of your revenues, even though they only make up about 20% of your customer base. I call that "The 80/20 Rule disappear. They move, they die off, they switch to another provider. Unless you have a plan in place to continue to grow your business beyond them, you will not have a viable future.

This means you need to continue to find more of those exact same kinds of top customers, the ones who are happy to keep buying from you and are financially able to make major purchases. It is easy to see how critical the search can be, especially when you keep in mind the 80/20 Rule.

Replacing your best customers, however, can be very challenging. Marketing to new customers is costly and difficult. Most businesses end up taking an old-school "Spray and Pray" approach, selling to everyone in an attempt to attract a couple of new big spenders. It is a huge waste, but most businesses do not see another choice. That is because they do not know who to market to, and as a result, they target everyone that happens to be on a generic marketing list that is grouped by income, zip code, or some other arbitrary criteria, even though 99.9% of those people will not become a new customer (let alone a lucrative new customer).

What if you could know exactly who to market your business to? What if you knew what your Ideal Customer's demographics were and could pinpoint with laser-like precision who these new red-hot leads were? That is where the real goldmine would be, right? Absolutely right!

Enter the Avatars

I have been tracking the success of marketing campaigns for my clients for quite a few years now and it has helped them zero in on what was successful so they could built on those successes. I must admit, I felt like it was still missing something from this process. These kinds of tracking systems primarily told you what marketing had worked. It provided a lot of rear-view mirror metrics that obviously are very important to anyone's marketing objectives, but nothing stands still forever. At some point, a business needs a roadmap for its future marketing, an integrated method of determining who are the best potential leads to target and how to find those targets. In other words, businesses needed a way to find more top customers to (a) increase existing revenues and (b) replace top customers who might exit.

I was driving around in my car one day, thinking about all this, when I realized the answer to the dilemma. It was pretty simple, really. What did the best existing customers of a business have in common? Were they mostly single or married? Did they have kids or not? High credit card usage or low? What was their discretionary spending like? How old were they? And so on.

Then came the all-important next step...

If I identified those traits, could I then target other leads that share those traits and successfully market to them? Would they be the prime candidates for the next wave of "best customers" for a business while creating a new wave of growth and revenue for that business? Could I, in fact, create "avatars" that would combine the dominant traits of these best customers and market directly to those leads who matched up with those avatars?

It was time to put my theory to the test. Once again, I turned to my very willing subject, my wife, the dentist. The first step was simple; I had to determine who her best customers were. As it turned out, The 80/20 Rule was confirmed: 20% of her patients were providing 80% of her income. That led me to the next stage, where my ROI Guy expertise really came in handy. She had over 61 million email addresses in her database that I could extract demographics from, which meant I could examine in detail the information of my wife's best customers and create an Avatar that contained the traits they had in common.

By the way, if you think you already *know* what kind of people your best customers are, you might want to wait until you actually know what your best customer Avatar looks like. In my wife's case, I asked her to guess what her best customers were like in all the important categories. She made what she thought was a good appraisal. Then I sprung the facts on her and she was shocked to find she was completely wrong; her best customers were actually the *opposite* from what she thought! It was another case of proving that, if you market on the basis of your assumptions instead of the facts, you may be completely off-track.

Anyway, it is not good for my marriage to dwell on my wife being wrong, so let me move on. From the data I discovered, I took the Avatar that represented her top customers and then cross-referenced it against the Avatars of many non-customer leads to see who matched up. In the process, I found *thousands of other people out there who were strikingly similar to that "best customer" Avatar.*

Once I created this list of potential "best customer" leads, I uncovered their physical street addresses, so I could target them with a special direct mail campaign from my wife's dental practice. I split that campaign into three different Avatars, depending on the specific demographics involved: [1] Empty Nesters (older couples whose kids had grown up and moved out), [2] Married Couples who were successful but did not have children, and [3] Very Successful Families, couples with children who were doing well financially.

This was exciting because, according to our figures, we were targeting people who spend 120 times more than the average customer. That is a pretty good basis for a marketing campaign, wouldn't you agree? Not only that, but through my Avatar selection process, I was also eliminating 90% of the traditional marketing list who were creating the ultimate "waste management" when it came to the cost of a campaign.

The more I thought about it, the cooler it seemed to be. Just as marketing tracking systems had eliminated the cost of marketing campaigns that do not work, now my Avatar system could eliminate the cost of marketing to leads that do not buy.

I went ahead and implemented the direct mail campaign to her special targeted "best customer" profile list and the results were astounding. Traditional response rates for dental direct mailings are anywhere from .05% to 2%, 2% being outstanding and considered to be successful results. The response rate on my wife's "best customer" profile list was over three times that top number—an awesome 7%!

I have not even mentioned another great bonus of this process. Since my ROI Guy crew had already done their demographic due diligence on these leads, we already had the access to critical information about them. That meant, when someone called my wife's dental office in response to a direct mailing, we would instantly be able to dig further into their data to determine how much in dental products and services they would qualify to buy.

Who Is Your Avatar?

Every business will have different Avatars that represent their top customers. Here is one I identified for a beauty salon:

Salon Avatar
- Women
- North Augusta and Aiken, SC
- Exhibits health and beauty buying behavior
- Interested in beauty and cosmetics
- Ages 36-65
- Household income of $150k +

And here are a couple more from a different dental practice:

Dental Practice Avatar #1
- Recently Divorced
- Women
- 5 mile radius from dental office
- Household income of $250k +

Dental Practice Avatar #2: "Soccer Moms"
- Married women
- 2+ kids
- Minivan driver
- Dog owner
- Household income of $150k +

Yes, I can actually identify potential leads who fit these specific Avatar profiles, thereby, allowing my clients to do more successful and focused targeted marketing that brings in new loyal customers.

The process begins with examining your customer/client database for the past two years and determining who has spent the most money with you. I then try to match thirty different demographics and categories to see what qualities these top customers share. Such factors as marital status, children, income, net worth, career-orientation (blue collar, white collar, professional, etc.), age, whether or not they are first-time home owners, etc. From that, I create your primary Avatar (your very best type of customer) and your secondary Avatar (your second-best type of customer).

From there, I can figure out who to market to, and I mean by their actual physical address. You do not have to send a direct mailing to every single person in a certain zip code, like in the old days (okay, not so old, just a few years ago!). Now, you can target individual homes and not waste time (and money) on marketing to those who probably are not going to respond to your pitch. There is no question that "one-size-fits-all" marketing is incredibly inefficient. Let Coke and Pepsi do the huge multi-million dollar image ads. Small and medium-sized businesses do not have that kind of marketing budget to throw around. Nor should they have to.

When you target the top-paying customers with this kind of precision, you are engaging in granular marketing on a whole new level. There may be only one person on a particular street in your area that might be the right person to sell your products and services to. With my Avatar techniques, I can find that person for you and you do not have to worry about anybody else on the block.

As Forbes Magazine put it, "This goldmine of data is a pivot-point moment for marketing and sales leaders. Those who are able to drive above-market growth, though, are the ones who can effectively mine that gold."

ROI Power Plays: Using Avatars to Your Advantage

Note: In these last few chapters, I am getting into areas where you may need assistance from a marketing professional to perform these particular ROI Power Plays, but here are a few things you might want to think about having done at your business:

Put the 80/20 Rule to the Test

How balanced or unbalanced is your customer revenue? Examine your database over the past few years and try to determine what percentage of your revenue your best customers contribute to your bottom line. Examine those top customers, if you know them well enough, to see what they have in common.

Determine Your Future Potential

Once you have had your top customer Avatars defined, a great next step is to examine your specific market to see how many of those types of leads are still out there to market to. You may find that you have a huge amount of folks who could be potential lucrative customers, or you may discover that you have already reached the bulk of your Avatars in your area and you have to either change up your products and services or maybe even relocate!

Pre-qualify Your Leads

As I noted earlier in this chapter, because we have all this data now at our fingertips, we can actually "score" those who match your Avatar profiles and find out just what they can and cannot afford. That way, when they do contact you about making a purchase, your staff can instantly find out exactly what their buying power is!

One final note about this process: these systems are used to determine who will be a good, profitable long-term customer. In other words, defining your Avatars is not about making one quick sale; it is about developing new loyal customers for life. The value of those kinds of clients is almost astronomical because they truly are the bedrock of your business.

In the next chapter, I am going to get into more specifics in terms of delivering the right message in the right way to your potential leads—by using the right technology!

Chapter 16
Matching Your Marketing with Your Target

Messaging and Placement that Hit the Bull's-eye

If you read the last chapter, you understand what I am talking about when I refer to who the main Avatars are when it comes to your customer base. In case you do not understand what I am talking about (it does happen), your Avatars represent the common pool of qualities that your top customers share. For example, maybe your most loyal customers are all green-eyed pharmacists who stutter. You do not know why, but that is what the numbers show. The next question is: how do you market the most effectively to those green-eyed pharmacists that have difficulty saying "Monsters make me miss my mom"?

There are two critical factors to zero in on when it comes to marketing to your specific Avatars and they are: (a) using the right media and (b) using the right message. When you do both of those things correctly, you cannot help but make a strong connection with your potential new customer.

Or, to put it another way:

ROI Guy Rule

When you talk as specifically as possible to your Avatars, they are a lot more likely to listen

---

Starting the Right Conversation

Let us pretend for a second that you are a stand-up comedian. Your agent has secured a booking for you and he gives you the address for the gig. He does not tell you anything else about the event. You decide to look as hip as possible, so you wear a torn t-shirt with some nasty words printed on the front with your skinny jeans and dirty sneakers. You prepare your most cutting-edge material, which includes lots of sex jokes and gross-out stories that involve bodily functions. In other words, the same routines every other comedian does. You know your stuff works and you are pumped up for a big night of laughs. When you pull up in front of the address the agent gave you, your heart sinks as you do a great big double-take. You have been booked at a Bible College and you instantly know you are headed for disaster.

Your "media"—the way you are dressed—is completely wrong for this crowd and so is your "message,"—your potentially-offensive material—it might work in a nightclub but it definitely is not going to cut it here. You have not tailored anything to this particular audience. You have no chance of connecting with them if you do your act; you quickly drive away and blow off the performance.

Switch out a marketer for the stand-up comic and you will understand exactly the kind of danger you can run into when you do not know who you are marketing to.

When you have not identified your Avatars and you implement a general one-size-fits-all marketing strategy, a lot of people on the receiving end of that strategy are going to instantly dismiss it for one reason or another. Too traditional. Not traditional enough. Too upper-class. Too lower-class, and so on and so forth. The fact is that there can be a million reasons people will feel that you must be talking to somebody else because you surely are not talking to them.

Finding the Right Media

Let me begin by talking about how to deliver your message to your specific target group, by giving you some detail on media that allow you to specifically reach your target group easily and effectively.

Direct Mail

For my money (and for yours, for that matter), the perfect way is through direct mail. Once you have defined your top customer Avatars, direct mail offers an unparalleled opportunity to target and segment your mailings to people who fit those Avatar profiles. Now, that might mean your mailing only goes to one particular person on a specific street, but that will be the *one* person you want to reach, so why waste your time and marketing budget on the others?

Lucky for all smart marketers, in the 21st Century, it is a simple matter to get a list of physical addresses of people within a ten mile radius of your business (or whatever size radius or area you want to zero in on) that match up as closely as possible to their Avatar profile. Why not take advantage of that technology and be a smart marketer yourself? Direct mail allows you to do that much better than any other vehicle.

Why? I have already touched on direct mail an earlier chapter, where I made the point that direct mail marketing is actually more effective than ever before. You might think the opposite is true since less people are actually using the mail for correspondence and bills these days; however, that is precisely why direct mail is so powerful now. The fact is people still go to the mailbox to get their mail, and they may find that the only piece of mail in their mailbox is YOURS. Consider the competitive advantage of that for a moment. Think about how many marketing emails cram your inbox during the day and how many you delete without even opening, because the numbers are so overwhelming. Consider how many commercials you see on TV or hear on the radio. Even putting an ad in the newspaper can get lost in the fine print.

By contrast, a direct mailing often stands by itself. Especially if you time it to arrive on a Tuesday (go ahead, check your mail on a Tuesday. If you are anything like me, frequently there is nothing there!).

A direct mailing also guarantees you a one-on-one audience with the recipient. He or she will look at your message without being distracted by anything else. An online ad, in contrast, is usually surrounded by tons of other content (especially since most browsers now effectively block pop-up ads).

One final point about the advantages of direct mail: Studies show that direct mail campaigns attract higher quality customers. These are customers who stay loyal longer and are more willing to buy higher-priced products and services.

Social Media

Social media sites also allow you to zero in on some aspects of your Avatars. For example, Facebook allows you to use targeted posts with a variety of different demographics including:

- Age
- Interests
- Relationship Status
- Gender
- Education Level
- Workplace

Currently, LinkedIn and Twitter also allow you to customize ads in similar ways.

There is some controversy about the effectiveness of these ads, as they often annoy users of the sites in question and cause them to lower their activity on them. Still, you have to remember that millions of potential customers use these services and it might be worthwhile to test the waters to see if they will work for you.

Other Online Marketing Methods

If you have ever looked for a product online, you have probably noticed that after you have used a search engine, ads for similar products begin appearing on web pages you visit. Obviously, this is a very effective way to reach someone who is actively interested in something you are selling.

You can also advertise directly with Google, Yahoo!, and other search engine companies. That way your ads either appear when someone searches on your keywords or your company shows up as a sponsored result at the top of the page.

These processes will not allow you to directly reach out to your Avatars, but they will allow you to directly reach "warm leads", people who are interested in your specific product or service.

Mobile Marketing

As I have previously talked about, Mobile marketing is becoming more and more important and it is easy to see why. Walk into any public place and take a look at how many people are staring at their Smartphones and walking into walls!

If you are able to reach your Avatar group on their mobile devices, either through social media or by actually texting to their phones, it can be very effective, especially if they are out shopping and actually making some buying decisions. Of course, that works better if you run a restaurant or a brick-and-mortar store, where someone is more likely to pop in on impulse, then if you run a medical clinic. However, reaching them on the road with a special offer that will get them in your door is always a powerful marketing move.

Facebook ads, by the way, also work better on mobile devices than, say, Google's, which can be hard to reach and click on.

In Person

Sometimes, because those who fit your Avatar profile have some strong interests in common, they will belong to the same group. What could be better than arranging with that group to do a free seminar or educational seminar on a subject that directly relates to your product or service?

What better way for you to personally connect with your most likely potential customers? It also affords the possibility of relating to them on a one-to-one level after you have finished speaking and started socializing.

For example, if you sell golf equipment or are a golf trainer, you might want to address a golfing association at a local country club. If you are a dentist who wants to market implants and dentures, you might want to speak at an upscale retirement community.

This approach can be incredibly potent and you have a great chance of making sales right in the room. The only danger here is that you market too hard and do not provide enough informational value in your talk. You must make sure you are giving them something of general interest, rather than relentlessly marketing what you sell.

Delivering the Right Message

In the previous section, I have given you a few very viable ways of reaching your Avatar target groups but, of course, the method of marketing is only half the battle.

The other half is creating the right message that will resonate with your particular group and convert them into becoming your customers. In a way, this is the easy part because you know you will be talking to a specific group of people with a specific group of traits. Most of the guesswork has been taken out of what can be an almost endless effort, where you try to cover all the angles for every conceivable group with one message. When you address a specific group, you are not forced to look for language that has to appeal to everyone; instead, you can talk to them directly in a way they want to listen to.

Unlike our hapless stand-up comic who showed up with his sex, drugs and rock n' roll routine at the Bible college, you know exactly who you are talking to. Let us take a look at a couple of Avatar scenarios and discuss how you could specifically tailor messages designed to appeal to them.

Dental Practice Avatar Example

This is an Avatar who we described in the last chapter as having the following qualities:

- Recently Divorced
- Women
- 5 mile radius from dental office
- Household income of $250k +

A divorced, upscale woman is most likely going to be concerned about making her appearance as attractive as possible, since she will be re-entering the dating pool. Your messaging should center on the great potential of her new life and how she will want to make sure her smile is as beautiful as possible. Since she lives close by to your practice, you will want to emphasize the convenience of becoming your patient, the newest procedures that can improve the appearance of her teeth and offer a free consultation if she wants to drop by.

Financial Planner Avatar

Now, suppose a financial planning firm has developed their own Avatar:

- Men
- 50+
- Household income of $300,000+
- 15 mile radius of office
- Homeowner

In that case, this is someone who is approaching retirement age, has plenty of disposable income and is probably concerned about saving enough for retirement. You will want to make an appeal to his enjoying his golden years without worrying about sacrificing his current level of lifestyle, or perhaps, to put his money in safe, stable investments that will not jeopardize the comfort of his post-working years.

In the above two instances, these are the basic messages you might want to deliver. You will want to deliver them a little more creatively and in a way that captures their interest, but it represents the gist of what you want to say.

As I have talked about before, you want to be *benefit-oriented* and focus on what your Avatars strongly desire and how the products and services you offer can provide it. Again, this is a lot easier to do when you are talking to a very specific group; take advantage of that and tailor your message to their wants and needs as much as possible!

ROI Power Plays: Plugging Directly into Your Avatars

Research Your Avatars

As noted, you have to know what your Avatars want and what they specifically respond to in order to market to them the most effectively. Therefore, do some research. You can hire a company that does demographic surveys, or you can talk to your customers who match up with the Avatars you want to market to. Ask them what they like best about your business and which products or services motivate them to patronize you and, while you are at it, question them about which marketing media they might respond to best.

The more you know about your Avatars, the better you can craft a specific message that pushes their buttons in the way you want them pushed. Before you plan the marketing do the research!

Test Your Messaging

You may come up with more than one creative marketing message for a particular Avatar. If this is the case, you may want to do what is called a "split test" and send each message to half of the people you want to reach to see which gets a better response rate. If both generate the same kind of sales, then, hey, you get to choose which one you like best!

You can also do a more informal test with those you know in the Avatar group to see if there is a consensus as to which messaging is more effective.

Compare Similar Target Marketing Methods

Odds are other businesses across the country that are similar to yours are marketing to similar Avatars. Join in a few professional organizations on LinkedIn or Facebook that are based in your particular industry and poll the members on what marketing tactics worked best on their Avatars. You might get some great secret tips and tricks to make your Avatar targeting pay off!

Once you identified your Avatars and decided on the best way to market to them, did it pay off? In our next chapter, I will reveal how to find out—to the penny—how well your marketing works! Turn the page for some more profitable reading.

Chapter 17
ROI Power Case Study Two

Dr. Scott D. Schumann, DDS, Grove City Dental

Scott, or "Schu" as he is known to his friends, runs a phenomenally-successful dental practice in the Columbus, Ohio area and attributes a lot of that success to his reliance on the marketing principles we are talking about in this section of the book. Here is his story:

When I tell people they should use Richard's amazing hi-tech marketing measurement techniques, I always add, "You're dumb if you don't do it," because there is no reason not to do it.

> *"You're dumb if you don't do it."*

I am already estimating he is going to save me $20,000 to $30,000 in marketing costs next year and I cannot even begin to describe how much he has increased my profits by using his new patient marketing and conversion services.

What I really like about Richard, besides the wonderful fact that he saves and makes me money, is that he provides me with all the latest and incredibly effective ROI tools that he develops. Richard provides real, concrete results that enable businesses like mine to make smart and informed marketing choices. You can actually see what you are doing wrong and right, for that matter, and act on that information.

Not only that, but Richard helps to keep my staff operating at the highest level possible. He allows all of us, even me, to see where we could be going wrong with patient interactions that might cost us a lot of business in the long-run. If you are open to what he and his partners have to tell you, then you are pretty much guaranteed to succeed.

I met Richard several years ago at a dental conference. His wife, Lisa, is also a dentist with a practice similar to mine and we often compare notes. While at the conference, Richard and I ended up hanging out in the back of the room talking (we were supposed to be listening to the speaker.). Up until then, I did pretty much the traditional marketing stuff most dentists do. I handed out Business cards, gave out toothbrushes with my name and number, advertised in the Yellow Pages and a little on the Internet, but not much.

Richard changed all that. When he began talking about using different phone numbers to track various marketing placements, I was amazed. I had never heard anything like this before. What you need to know about me is that I fought very hard to get a great easy-to-remember phone number for Grove City Dental: "801 1000". I was in love with that number and really proud that I managed to get it. While the tracking number concept seemed exciting, it was hard to let go of good old "801 1000." Ultimately, I did let it go and once I began seeing the results, I suddenly did not care if my once-beloved phone number disappeared altogether.

Thanks to his ROI Matrix system, incoming sales calls to the tracking numbers that he has assigned to my practice are automatically recorded and the caller's name and address are inputted into the software database, where we can instantly access them. This information can be used again later to market a follow-up campaign.

This was a godsend. Yes, my staff used to tell me they were manually collecting all this data when they answered phone calls. However, when Richard began monitoring our calls, he told me that this was not the case. Nothing against my staff, after all, they won "Best Team" in a nationwide contest, so I certainly know they are top-notch. It is merely a human thing and, as I am quick to admit, I was as guilty as anyone of not writing down important contact information from a caller interested in our services.

Thanks to Richard's system, nothing slips through the cracks. Not only that, we can access those recorded incoming sales calls through Richard's website and go over what we did right and what we did wrong. With that kind of instant review, my staff actually enjoys listening to them and pointing out their own mistakes. As long as it is a positive learning experience, nobody takes it personally.

One service we used from Richard was the Video Mystery Patient: Basically, someone calls pretending to be a new patient and books an appointment with us. That person comes in, armed with a tiny video camera on their person, and secretly tapes the entire experience, from the greeting by my receptionist to my interaction with them.

This is where I was proudest of our operation at my practice. When the "mystery patient" arrived, after making an appointment in advance, we had no idea he was the plant. He ended up actually paying for treatment from us and is now one of our regular patients, even though he lives about an hour away from our offices. That is right! *We converted the guy who was supposed to test how good our conversion was.* It does not get much better than that.

Back to Richard's tracking phone numbers. We used them in tons of places. For instance, We put tracking numbers on the backs of folding chairs we donated to an Ohio State football tailgate party and we even made one of our staff's cell phone number our tracking number one weekend for a special campaign, so she could book appointments remotely when the office was closed!

We have a lot of fun using the tracking numbers in every conceivable way and when I say every conceivable way, I mean it. I golf and I am not a patient golfer. I like to hit the ball and, as I like to say, learn not to suck at it as much. When I lose a ball by hitting it into the rough, I do not go looking for it. I get out a new ball and continue on with my game. Losing all those balls got me to thinking: I should be able to get something out of all those lost balls, after all, I am sure other people find them and they end up with a great freebee. I decided to put the Grove City Dental logo on the balls I use, along with one of Richard's magic tracking numbers. The best part is that it worked and we actually have gotten calls from golfers who found my lost golf balls!

On the serious side, Richard has also been invaluable in helping me market to my "Avatars." With Richard's tracking numbers I can quickly find out which campaign is working with these kind of potential clients and which one is not. I can test which headline works on an internet or print ad and which one does not. I can even try out different online videos with different tracking numbers.

I really look at Richard as an incredible resource and a real marketing partner. Whenever I need a new tracking number for a new placement, all I have to do is pick up the phone and he is there with one. He has helped me and my staff become as good as we can possibly get at marketing and customer service. It has paid off in so many ways that I have lost count.

Chapter 18
Tracking, Measuring and Analyzing

How to Get a Dollar Back for Every Dime Spent

Okay, it is time to make some money.

That probably comes as a relief to many of you who have been reading this book and thinking to yourselves, "This is all well and good, but what does it do for my bank account?" The answer is, more than you ever imagined. As I have already mentioned, I more than doubled my wife's dental practice revenues in less than a year through the techniques you have learned, and will continue to learn, in this book.

These techniques involve using proven scientific marketing systems that eliminate the guesswork and focus on tangible, knowable profits. The fact is that too many small and medium-sized businesses traditionally rely on guesswork to do their marketing because they do not understand (a) how affordable tracking their marketing actually is and (b) how much profit it can generate.

This kind of thinking almost killed the most powerful being on the planet. Yes, I am talking about, The Man of Steel himself, Superman. Let us journey back to 1939, when comic books were in their infancy and the internet might have been something you only saw in a Flash Gordon movie. That is the year that "Action Comics" published its first issue and the very first superhero named (what else?) Superman was on the cover for the very first time.

Only one problem. The publisher would not know for about six months whether Superman was actually a hit or not, because that is how long it took for the newsstands to report back to the distributors and the distributors to report back to the publisher. Since Superman was such a new idea for the time, the publisher could not count on it being an instant success, or any kind of success at all, for that matter. The publisher, forced to "market in the dark," featured other stories on the cover of "Action Comics", Tarzan rip-offs, spy sagas, war adventures, etc. because he had no idea whether Superman was anything anyone cared about. In time, he began to hear about kids haunting the stores asking for more of those Superman comics and decided he might have a good thing going. Unfortunately, it was not until issue 7 that the publisher could take advantage of his new hit character and that the Man of Steel reappeared on the cover.

Yes, Superman turned out to be the super-success story of the century but the publisher still left a lot of money on the table because he could not know that he had discovered the biggest sensation in comics' history.

Superman is a property that continues to pay off to this day. In 2013, he was in the blockbuster Man of Steel movie and the producers knew on opening day they had a winner. Why? They knew because they could instantly track how many people bought tickets!

In this chapter, I am going to show you the way many of my clients track their marketing and why it has become so important to their bottom line. First, let me start off with this chapter's rule:

ROI Guy Rule

When you know how much money each campaign

makes – you know how to make a lot more!

How It Works

You have probably read some descriptions of how a marketing tracking system works in some of the case studies I have included in this book. Let me walk you through it so you understand how simple this kind of system is to put into action and how easy it is to use. I am going to specifically be discussing how my ROI Matrix tracking system works for the purposes of this chapter.

First of all, the simplest way to track your marketing, especially offline marketing, is to use a separate and unique contact phone number on each campaign. For example, if you send a coupon mailing, the coupon has its own tracking phone number. Your appointment card would have a different tracking phone number as would your newspaper ad, and so forth.

Even though the phone numbers are different, they are all linked to the same ultimate destination, whatever phone line you designate. It could be your office number, an answering service or automatic response system (I will talk more about in the next chapter). In other words, the various phone numbers are only different when it comes to their digits; they all end up at the same destination number.

The reason for the difference is to allow the ROI Matrix to directly link each incoming sales call to the campaign or item that generated it. I will use "Ellen Jones" as an example. Ellen sees an ad for cosmetic dentistry and, using the phone number on the ad, calls the dental practice to find out more. The tracking software picks up that Ellen is calling as a result of the ad and notes it in its data collection.

It is also able, in most cases, to identify that someone named Ellen Jones is on the other line and instantly load her contact information into the system without your staff having to lift a finger. (I will talk about why that is important in the next chapter.)

Whoever answers Ellen's call will be sent an email after the call is completed, prompting the staff person to enter into the system whether (1) Ellen Jones is a genuine lead (i.e., if she is interested in any of your products and services) and (2) if she made an appointment or a purchase.

This lead continues to be tracked down the line in order to ultimately know how much Ellen Jones ended up buying from the business in question. Whatever profit is made gets attributed to the marketing campaign that prompted her to call in the first place.

Now, as other people call as a result of different campaigns and marketing placements, the same process occurs. The tracking system continues to tabulate how many leads were generated by each campaign and how much money the campaign brought in as a result.

Below I have placed a screen grab from the Matrix to illustrate how the real-time data gets displayed to the business owner (or any staff member who is authorized to access the Matrix information). I have omitted the specific phone numbers and business names due to privacy issues, but the rest of the information is the real deal. These are only a few of the specific campaigns being tracked in this case.

Ads Data (07/17/13 - 08/16/13)

Marketing Ad / Campaign	Leads	Calls	Appointments	Cost	ROI	Production	Collected	Actions
Referral	42	0	38	$1.00	$43,859.15	$11,975.76	$0.00	
Main Office Line	38	512	24	$0.00	$0.00	$0.00	$0.00	
Save On Postcard	38	50	14	$2,800.00	$20,076.00	$1,964.00	$1,216.00	
Save On	31	32	12	$2,565.00	$-1,520.00	$1,022.00	$941.00	
WEB	28	220	20	$50.00	$36,935.36	$4403.36	$0.00	
Referral	28	1	28	$1.00	$50,404.31	$18,623.33	$5653.80	
Referral	27	0	27	$1.00	$78,071.00	$21,813.00	$8,980.00	
DelCor Atoka	19	59	15	$100.00	$50,637.29	$3,823.07	$0.00	
Referral	18	0	17	$1.00	$25,878.16	$3,704.16	$0.00	
Dentist Sapulpa	17	0	13	$0.00	$79,784.51	$10,995.43	$0.00	

Showing 1 to 10 of 219 entries

As you can see, the ROI Matrix gathers the following data on each campaign:

- How many leads were generated

- How many calls were made as a result of the campaign

- How many calls resulted in actual appointments

- The cost of the marketing campaign

- The amount sold to the lead

- The amount paid to date

And most importantly...

- *The actual ROI of the campaign* (the money made from the campaign verses the money spent on the campaign)

This can lead to some shocking discoveries. For instance, in the screen grab, check out the Referral campaign. Cost? $1.00. ROI? $78,071. I would say that is a pretty worthwhile campaign!

By contrast, take a look at the "Save On" campaign in the screen grab. That cost over $2500 to put into motion. However, the ROI at this point in time is a negative $1520, since the campaign only brought in around $1000. NOT a worthwhile campaign!

It's Not What It Costs, It's What It Makes

The previous point illustrates a critical marketing concept: do not confuse how much money a campaign costs with how much it might make. The reality is that there is absolutely no correlation between the two numbers, except maybe in a marketer's mind. Sometimes we want to feel like a big shot and plunk down a few grand for a giant billboard, thinking it is going to bring in all kinds of money. It might, but it might not. If you are a small business, can you afford that gamble?

The beauty of tracking your marketing campaigns is that gambling begins to disappear from your marketing strategies. You discover that sometimes the cheapest possible marketing can bring in incredible results, while expensive marketing can end up costing you. However, you never know that unless you track your marketing. It is the only way you can be sure you know what is working for you.

There are some people who regard marketing tracking as an additional service they cannot afford. You might even be one of those people. After all, every penny has to count and you have to make sure that it does. The thing is that tracking your marketing actually makes you a lot more money by enabling you to target your marketing dollars in the most effective way. On the other hand, if you do not measure your ROI by tracking your marketing expenditures, you could literally be throwing money away just when you need to maximize spending effectiveness the most.

What is the point of advertising when you have no idea if are reaching the right target group, or if your ad concept is having the right impact on your intended audience? Tracking your marketing means you can spend smarter and boost revenues at the same time. Aren't those your ultimate goals?

Answering the All Important Questions

Most importantly, tracking your marketing answers critical questions about your media and your messaging, answers you need to know in order to sell your products and services in the most powerful and effective ways possible. I will take a moment to talk about those products and services.

Can you imagine not knowing the Who, What, When and Where, let alone the Why, of the product or service you are selling? Sounds ridiculous, right? To me, it is ridiculous not to be able to answer those questions about your marketing, especially if you spend a large amount of time, money and effort on it. Without tracking the marketing, you do not know who you are reaching, what you are accomplishing, when and where to do your marketing or why it works or does not work. That is not a great way to approach, frankly, anything.

Tracking your marketing can tell you:

WHO...
...is responding to your marketing? You can find out by using a combination of tracking/lead capture toll-free hotline that automatically builds your business an incredible marketing database of already interested prospects.

WHAT...
...campaigns, copy and visuals are most effective at bringing in customers? Least effective? Tracking answers to those questions enables you to hone in on the products, services and advertising approaches that generate the most cash.

WHERE...
...is the best place to advertise your particular product or service? Radio? Bus stop benches? Direct mail? Or Google AdWords? You will find out instantly when you begin tracking your marketing because you will know

exactly where those prospects are coming to you from, without having to rely on their hit-or-miss memory.

WHEN...

...is your marketing most effective? Is there a time of year when your product or service is most appealing and you should market more heavily? Is there another time of year when it is not even worth any marketing money or effort? Again, tracking provides hard answers.

WHY...

...has your marketing not been as effective as it should be? Why do you often feel like you are throwing money out the window when you spend it on marketing because the results are not there?

You can measure your marketing ROI like you can measure anything, and ROI tracking systems will do the trick every time. They help ensure your advertising makes as much impact as possible and reaches as many potential customers as possible.

By properly using tracking and lead capture systems, you can easily increase your marketing and advertising ROI. Studies show they boost your marketing results dramatically because when you finally know the answers to all 5 of those big W's, you avoid mistakes and make the smartest, most informed moves that you can.

I know they say, *"If it ain't broke, don't fix it."* You may agree with that, because your business is profitable, your marketing "ain't" broke. You can still drive a little ways on a flat tire, but at some point, you are going to get stuck. Your marketing and advertising could be like that flat tire and you may think your business is riding along just fine. Sooner or later, if you do not track your marketing to make sure it is pumping up your profits, you may find your business is suddenly going nowhere.

To bottom-line this: Business is all about *making more than you spend,* correct? The whole point of determining your marketing ROI is just that, to make more than you spend on your advertising. When you tabulate your ROI automatically through a tracking system, you can make sure you are working with the correct numbers. You might try to rely on your staff to try and gather that information, but that is an incredibly time-consuming, and often impossible, task.

A marketing tracking system allows you to monitor your marketing like a giant corporation, without spending the insane amounts of money they do. Technology has progressed to the point where you can have this invaluable information literally at your fingertips, with just a few keystrokes. My clients have access to an exclusive online portal that calculates, in real time, their marketing ROI numbers, and they can make important and profitable decisions based on those numbers.

You can make a dollar for every marketing dime you spend. As you saw in the case of the referral campaign, you can even make $82,000 for every dollar! The point is you cannot know where your money is coming from without marketing tracking data. As your Avatars point you to the kind of customer that will make you the most money, tracking systems point you to the marketing that will make you the most money. Isn't that the direction you want to be pointed in?

ROI Power Plays: Tracking Your Marketing Success

Decide If It's the Medium or the Message

A campaign's marketing success, or failure, will depend on its message or how you deliver that message. Those are the two important factors, as I have emphasized throughout this book. The longer you track marketing, the easier it will be able to determine whether it is one or the other. For example, if a type of online advertising has always been very effective but, when you change the content, the response suddenly falls off, you can probably blame the changed messaging. In any case, test your messages through the cheapest possible campaigns to test their effectiveness, and then commit more money to them once you know they pack some power. Go through the same process when you try out a new media. Use a proven message and see how your results come out.

Keep Up Your Reach

Once you start tracking your marketing, you may be tempted to focus on the one or two campaigns with the highest ROIs. Before you do that, remember that different campaigns reach different segments of your potential customers and, as long as a campaign is profitable, you might want to keep more in the mix. Naturally, you want to eliminate marketing that does not make you money, but there is no reason not to spend more to make more, if it fits in with your overall strategy.

Not All Marketing Is About Sales

You should also consider, especially if you are a business that depends on your local community's good will, spending money on marketing that might not bring back immediate sales, but will bolster your neighborhood profile. Sponsoring high school sports teams, street festivals and so forth are expense items that will strengthen your branding, even if they do not bring in immediate revenue. Then again, they might. Continue to use tracking numbers for these types of sponsorships as well!

In the next chapter, I will cover the inner workings of a marketing tracking system, in more depth. I will explain how to track which campaigns are bringing in the most leads and why that can be very beneficial to your bottom line!

Chapter 19
ROI Power Case Study Three

Jeff Giagnocavo, Owner, Gardner's Mattress and More

For the past two-plus years, Jeff Giagnocavo has been the owner of Gardner's Mattress and More, located in Lancaster, Pennsylvania. He has been working with our ROI Matrix and Database DNA tools for about a year now. His results? Well, I will let him drop the details on you. This is a case study I'm incredibly proud of.

I met Richard Seppala when he was speaking at an event and I was

> "Without the ROI Matrix, we would be throwing money into the wind, hoping it sticks."

blown away by the amount of intelligence that he can mine from both your list of current customers as well as your list of prospects. At the time, I was struggling with how to do my marketing efficiently. I had a list of close to 13,000 customers, and I could not possibly afford to send direct mail to all of them because it would end up putting me out of business. That's what made me want to work with Richard and his services.

That process began with sending him our marketing list so he and his team could score it. From the list, he calculated the demographics of our ideal "avatars", the types of customer who were giving us the most business. Wouldn't you know it, the old 80/20 rule applied, in that the consumers who made up 20% of our base were providing us with 80% of our revenue.

We came up with 5 main avatars and, based on that, we replicated those to come up with a prospect list in our local area that we could market to. Right now, we are working in teams from a small list of 500 prospects who are our "best of the best," when it comes to potential customers. We are not only communicating with our best customers, we are only spending our dollars on these best customers. Without the ROI Matrix, we would not be able to do that. We would be throwing money into the wind, hoping it sticks.

Our results have really been great, especially the savings from segmenting our marketing list. Also invaluable have been Richard's telephone tracking numbers. We are using about 28 of them at the moment. Recently, we had a client calling us, looking for a latex bed. We had a great conversation on the phone, about a half-hour talk, and I let him know we would send him out some information.

I then looked at the instant analysis of him that was provided by Richard's scoring system, and realized he fit the profile of one of our top 5 avatars. He was in Elizabethtown, and, what do you know, my service guy was going to Elizabethtown that same day to handle an issue for somebody else! I grabbed my service guy and said, "Hey John, drop this off; put it in the front door." The potential customer was blown away by our package, called later that afternoon and I ended up making an $8000 sale in three days, as opposed to having to wait to follow up in a week or so and risk losing that customer to somebody else. By the way, that $8000 was double what the guy was planning on spending.

The tracking numbers pay off in a lot of amazing ways. We put them on our Yellowbook ads, our website and giveaways. We can measure the ROI of those different marketing efforts, thanks to the tracking numbers. We can say, "Okay, we spent $5000 on that campaign and had $50,000 in sales, we know that is a 10 to 1 return on investment, it is worth doing again." The tracking numbers also show that we are getting a ton of pull from our Yellowbook ads. In this day and age, people might think that is odd, but we are doing them right and our competition is leaving the stage.

The tracking numbers really lead to surprises. There was a local food and wine festival, very high-end, about a hundred bucks for a pair of tickets just to get in. That is the kind of clientele I want to be in front of, therefore, I had a booth there. I made up a nice little package to put in everybody's bag and all my stuff had different tracking numbers. The bad surprise was that most of the stuff I gave out did not bring us back any leads. The good surprise was that I had notepads made up in the shape of a wineglass and put a tracking number on that, and discovered that item, more than any other, had the biggest pay-off. That taught me, do not go full-out giving a big expensive package to everybody, because they may not care. Instead, only do the notepads. Hand them out like candy, and create a lot of engagement.

Another thing I am doing this year to take advantage of the ROI Matrix's abilities is working with a local baseball team. It is a club team, not affiliated with any major league team, but they get about 4500 people going to each of their games. They play 70 home games, that is about a quarter million eyeballs coming through the stadium and I wanted to take advantage of those numbers.

I was given the opportunity to advertise on the huge right field banner with one of my vendors, the Serta Mattress Company. I gave them a brief presentation on how I was going to use the ROI Matrix, together with my GenSoft marketing database program, because Richard created the Matrix to work very tightly with these kinds of programs. I showed them how I could instantly score prospects who responded, determine whether they were worth marketing to and put them through a follow-up marketing system that would most likely produce about 120 sales at about $2000 a piece, close to a quarter of a million dollars in revenue over the entire baseball season. All I was asking Serta for was $16,000 to pay for the banner placement. They agreed because everything I showed them was based on hard numbers.

The fact that incoming sales calls are recorded through the Matrix is also a big help. I can make sure my people are saying the right thing on the phone, getting the contact information, and taking the opportunity to advance the prospect forward to buying.

I cannot recommend Richard's services enough. I have had a 20% month-to month growth this year and The ROI Matrix is a part of that growth. Anybody that is marketing today, if you are not using a system like The ROI Matrix, you are fooling yourself. Big Brother data is going to get bigger. The Matrix is one of those tools that keeps working on your business, even when you do not have the time to do it yourself. You do not have to do it, it will do it for you.

Chapter 20
No Stones Unturned

Diving Deeper into Marketing Tracking

Okay, it is time to make you some *more* money and, as a bonus, show you some visuals that will blow your mind (do not worry, no LSD is involved!).

In the last chapter, I talked about how to track your marketing to make sure you know which media and message brings in the most profits because it makes perfect sense that you would want to eliminate the guesswork.

In this chapter, I will delve further into everything tracking your marketing can reveal about your business. That way you can see for yourself, first-hand, the kind of information these systems can deliver. In other words....

ROI Guy Rule

Tracking your marketing unlocks many "data doors" that open you up to a whole new world of profit!

The Nuts and Bolts of Marketing Tracking

So far, I have only given you a little peek into what a marketing tracking system can show you, instantly and in real time, through your own exclusive online portal. As I said, in this chapter, I am going to tunnel deeper into the inner workings of an automated system such as my ROI Matrix.

Ready? Let us start burrowing...

If you look at the following screen shot (which, again, is missing specific names, phone numbers and businesses for privacy reasons), you will see how you can keep track of how many legitimate leads call over a certain time period. Not only that, you can keep track of your conversion rate, i.e., how many lead calls actually resulted in a sale or, at the very least, an appointment. Why is that important to note? Conversion rates tend to stay fairly consistent, therefore, if there is a sudden drop-off, you need to address it (and, with a system like this, it is easy to do. See Dr. Kelly Brown's case study in this section for more on that).

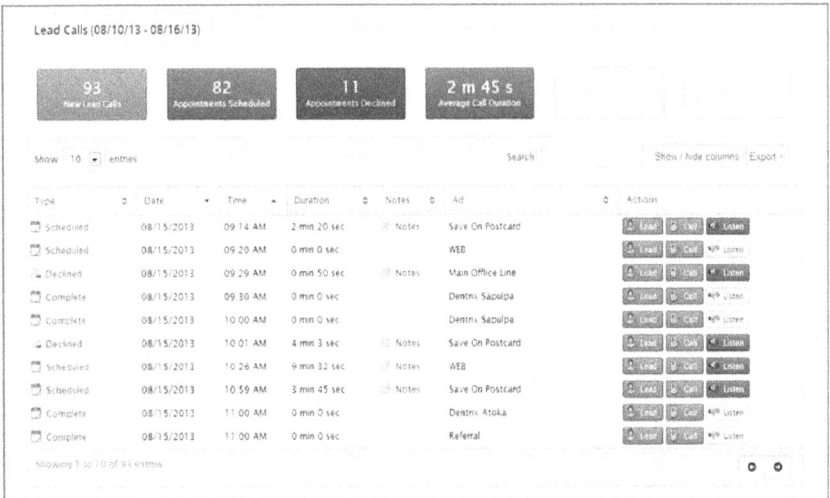

Notice the column to the very right of the screenshot where you will see a little "Listen" button for each phone call. By clicking that button, you can (a) easily access a recording of every single incoming sales call online at your convenience and (b) check those calls to see if the staffer who is handling them is doing a good job enticing leads to actually buy from you. If that staffer is not, you can either try to train them to do better or perhaps rotate someone else into that critical position.

The point is you can instantly see if you have a problem with the way your incoming sales calls are being handled and you can instantly address it. You cannot do that if you do not have the hard data to make an accurate judgment; otherwise you are depending on whatever your staff tells you is going on, or on your own personal hunches. That means that problem could continue, or even grow worse. Either way, it will cost you a lot in sales over the long haul.

A call tracking system can feed you other important information. Check out the two screenshots that follow. The first screenshot breaks down the number of calls from leads (and non-leads) by time of day. The second screenshot breaks it down by day of the week. Again, you can detect patterns; for instance, you can see from the second screenshot that more lead calls come in on Monday and Wednesday. That is important information which can help you plan your office schedules to take advantage of those patterns.

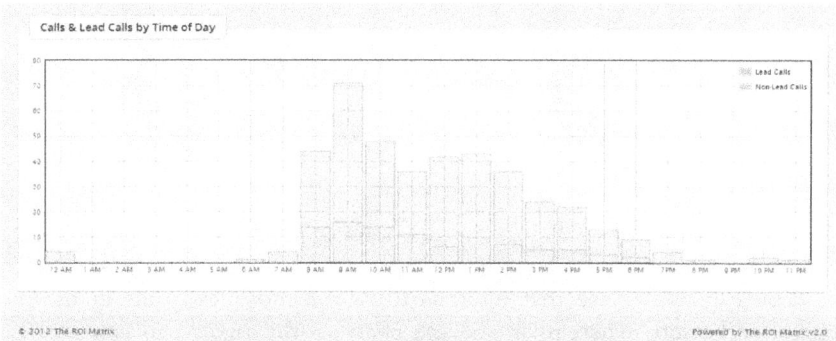

Which Marketing is Bringing in the Most Customers?

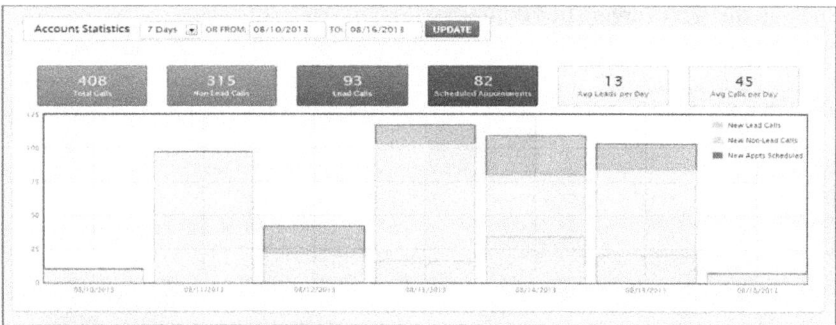

If you are interested in developing viable leads to market to (and who is not?), you will also want to know more about which of your campaigns do the best at a particular task. Luckily, a solid marketing tracking system will do that for you as well, and once again, deliver the critical information at a glance.

Some campaigns, for one reason or another, prompt a lot of calls, but not from people who, realistically, are going to become customers. As a matter of fact, they may be salespeople who are trying to get you to buy from them. Therefore, you also want to know which campaigns are driving the most calls that are not from potential customers, in other words, non-leads.

Here is an example of how my ROI Matrix breaks down that information for you:

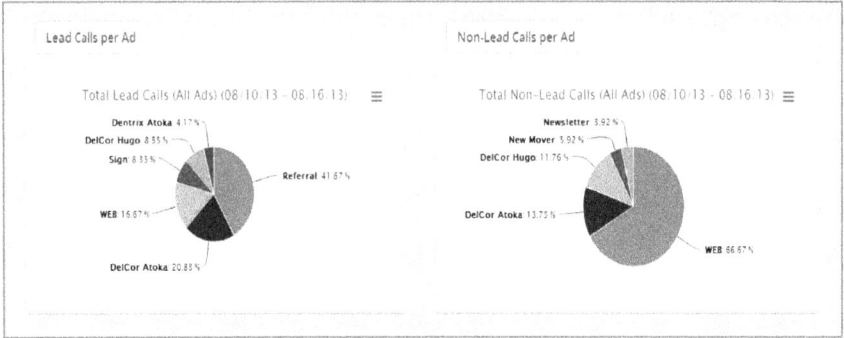

You can clearly see that referrals drive the most lead calls in the pie chart to the left, whereas, in the pie chart to the right, you can see the internet drives the most non-lead calls (probably because it is the easy way to look up the business number).

Speaking of the internet, online marketing is, of course, a huge component of anyone's advertising efforts. That is why you need to make sure any tracking system you consider delivers the right online data too, such as the next screenshot demonstrates:

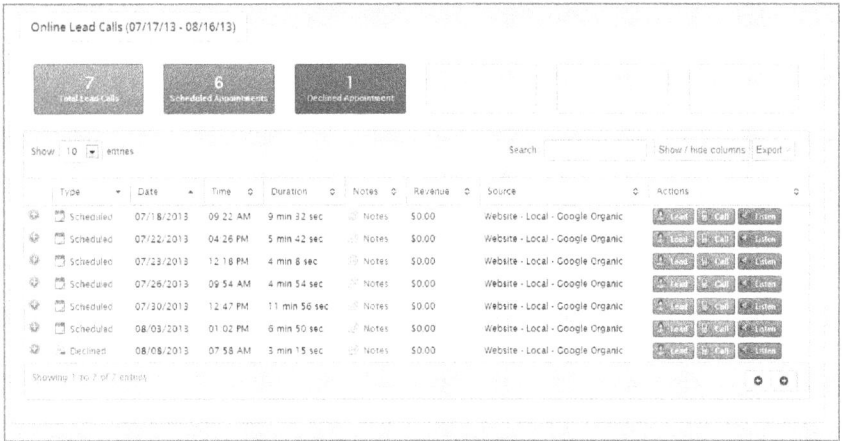

Here, you are able to see how many lead calls your website is generating and how many conversions you are getting out of those calls (you can, of course, track any online ad campaign the same way as any other marketing campaign).

Additionally, you can see which online keywords are working best for you. Here is a sample screenshot from my wife's dental ROI Matrix account that demonstrates how that works:

When you use a tracking system such as The ROI Matrix to break down which campaigns are delivering the most profitable leads, you can further fine-tune your marketing strategy to increase your revenues.

This system is easily customized to show you the data you want to see when you want to see it. The previous screens are only examples of how some of my clients work with The ROI Matrix to uncover what they want to know about how to make their marketing more effective and more profitable.

Again, tracking your marketing makes it easy as pie to access this data with a few keystrokes. When you are not tracking your marketing in this kind of automatic, systematic manner, you are either working overtime to gather it (inaccurately, in most cases) on your own, or you are back in the land of guesswork, which is where no business person should ever make their residence!

ROI Power Plays: Doing Deep Marketing Analysis

Keep Your Staff Sharp with Call Recordings

Having your incoming sales calls recorded is an awesome way to continuously train your staff in how to best establish a relationship with a new lead and "seal the deal" in terms of making a purchase or an appointment. By regularly (weekly at most or monthly at least) sitting down and reviewing some of the calls with them, you can discuss, in a positive and non-threatening way, why some conversions failed and why some succeeded. Since they may not like hearing themselves on these recordings, keep it light and keep it focused on the task of improving their sales abilities. That way, it will not be an ordeal for you or them!

Determine Your Top Lead Times

As I noted in this chapter, you can discover patterns to the time of day, as well as the day of the week, when you get the most incoming sales calls from new leads. Take advantage of that data by making sure your best sales staff member is on the phones during those times and that a live person is always on hand to take those calls. You do not want to rely on voicemail during those times because you want to optimize your opportunity to sell to a "hot" lead, someone who is interested enough in your products and/or services to actually pick up the phone and call!

Compare online to offline results.

More and more people are making buying decisions online, often with their mobile devices (tablets, Smartphones, etc.) in hand.

This is an important trend for any marketer to keep track of, especially since, very often, offline campaigns cost more than online ones, depending on which ones you are using. In any event, track on an ongoing basis the results of your online marketing verses. Your offline marketing and, if you see dramatic shifts heading to the internet, adjust your strategy accordingly.

In our next and final chapter, I am going to talk about capturing and keeping a lead for life. When you calculate the actual value of a lifetime customer, it ends up being a huge number. Stay tuned and find out how to keep growing your pool of always-loyal buyers!

Chapter 21 The ROI Lifecycle

Keeping a Lead for Life with "The Magic Pill"

So far, in this section of the book, I have been focusing almost exclusively on tracking marketing campaigns. That is only part of the big picture, however. What is just as important, if not even more important, *is to track your leads.*

Why? Let us review some important statistics from earlier, where we talked about how crucial follow-up marketing is:

- 2% of sales are made on the first contact
- 3% of sales are made on the second contact
- 5% of sales are made on the third contact
- 10% of sales are made on the fourth contact
- 80% of sales are made on the fifth to twelfth contact

In other words, one of the biggest marketing mistakes you can make, after you get a viable lead, is to stop marketing to that person if they do not buy from you right away. Since, many of you reading this book run small or medium-sized businesses or practices, you do not have a lot of time or resources to devote to following up on these leads in the way they should be, or you do not market to them correctly in the first place. These deficiencies end up losing you an awful lot of money. I am not talking a little money, I am repeating, an *awful lot of money.* Nobody wants to do that! At least nobody I know.

In this last chapter, I am going to talk briefly about tracking your leads and how that enables you to keep them buying from you for a lifetime. That is why this chapter's ROI Guy Rule is:

ROI Guy Rule

Automatically track your leads
and market to them until they "buy or die."

129

Following the Leads

The phrase "buy or die" in the ROI Guy Rule may sound more than a little ominous to you readers, but I do not mean to insinuate you are going to have to market to people until they end up six feet under. By "die," I mean you market to them until it is obvious they are no longer a viable lead because they have either (a) moved (b) found another provider or (c) simply requested to be removed from your marketing list.

Until that "fatal" moment comes when they are no longer a potential lead, there is no reason you cannot keep making contact (I call each moment of contact a "touch") with someone who has demonstrated an interest in what you have to sell. You can continue to generate simple "touches" (such as sending out a postcard or an email) *automatically and affordably* and barely lift a finger doing it. You only need to have the right system in place. For instance, this is how it works when using my ROI Matrix system. Whenever you identify a lead through the tracking system, their available contact information which is obtainable through the phone number they are calling from, is automatically added to, not only the Matrix program, but also your company's own personal CRM (Customer Relationship Management software). You can, of course, also add the lead information manually. Here is a look at a blank lead information form from the Matrix:

This is merely the upper section of the form, there are more information boxes that, once filled in, keep all that critical information at your fingertips. You can input the source of the lead, the date the lead contacted you, and score how good the lead is on a scale from 1 to 5 (for example, a lead that buys something expensive right off the bat is obviously a "5," whereas someone just looking for a freebee might be a "0."). There are also boxes for contact information, such as address, phone number and email address, as well as a box where you can input general information, such as specific products and services they bought or are interested in.

The lead information form gives you a very important option at the bottom:

See those colored boxes at the bottom? That is where you can choose to uncover their "Digital DNA" through the Matrix. When you select that option, you can potentially discover at least two important facts:

- The "Avatar" attributes the leads possesses (in order to see if they fall into one of your top customer demo clusters, as discussed in Chapter 14)

- How much they can afford to spend with you (you can see how important that can be in the Jeff Giagnocavo case study in this section of the book)

If you have read the entire book up until this point, and I hope you did, you will know how important those two points are. I will spell it out here:

- The first piece of data could indicate the lead fits the profile of *the best possible potential customer* for your business. If the lead matches up with one of your Avatars, then they are likely to be more receptive to your marketing, spend more money with you and stay loyal to your business longer. Those are all very good things.

- The second piece of data is a matter of scoring their credit and past purchase history. It pre-qualifies them in terms of spending power, which, again, is another crucial piece of information to have because you know what they are capable of buying and what you can reasonably offer to them, in terms of a product or service they might require.

Again, for the importance of that data, I refer you to the case study of Jeff Giagnocavo, the owner of Gardner's Mattress and More, where he was able to "score" the buying power and Avatar status of one of his incoming sales calls leads, and immediately act to secure a sale of thousands of dollars, *all because he could access that information immediately*. When you track your leads through a system such as The ROI Matrix, you automatically have their contact data, their buying history with you and their Database DNA. You know what they are interested in buying, what they have bought, and how much they can afford to spend. You know just like Jeff Giagnocavo did, whether they are worth spending a few extra bucks in marketing on, in order to sell them a higher-level item.

The Magic Pill

Since I call my tracking system, The ROI Matrix, I named a special feature of it, "The Magic Pill." That is because, if you recall from the movie, *The Matrix*, you needed to take a pill to fully immerse yourself into that artificial reality.

In order to fully immerse yourself in all the marketing possibilities of a tracking system like mine, I believe you also have to take a pill, and to me, because of the enchanting results it creates, it is definitely a *Magic Pill*.

The Magic Pill was created to continue to keep your leads in The ROI Lifecycle, in other words, to keep them coming to you as long as they are buying whatever your business sells (or chooses to sell in the future).

Most business owners do not have the time, energy or manpower to follow up on leads as they should. That is why I realized that the more you automated the process, the more companies and practices would take advantage of the hands-free aspects of it. That way they could:

- continually market to viable leads
- keep contact with people who may have stopped buying for one reason or another
- retain and upsell to the customers they already had.

And they could do all that without a lot of time and effort.

To put it simply, I designed The Magic Pill to be a *completely-automated marketing sequence* designed to convert prospects into lifelong customers/clients or patients, without you or your staff lifting a finger (well, maybe a couple of fingers to enter a few facts online). It ensures that a potentially-valuable lead does not get lost in the shuffle, through a series of marketing messages that are:

- Automatic
- Personalized

- Targeted
- Situation-specific

For example, at a dental practice, a lead might call and not make an appointment. Or make an appointment and not show up. Or come in for a consultation and not buy. Often that is the end of it.

With The Magic Pill, it actually is the *beginning*, because it *continues* to communicate with that lead through emails, postcards and other mailings, with messages designed to convert that prospect into a paying patient.

If you revisit Chapter 12, you will find a lot of important information about follow-up marketing, such as setting up a sequence of "touches" to continue marketing to a client, which might include an email auto-responder sequence. The Magic Pill incorporates those marketing musts in an automated system that saves you work and makes you more profits.

All this helps you to avoid falling into the trap many businesses do. They build their customer bases up to a certain level and feel good about their revenue stream. Unfortunately, that customer base at some point will move on for various reasons and the business is left scrambling to keep its doors open.

Automating your campaign tracking and follow-up marketing enables you to keep a steady stream of new customers buying from you and also is a big boost to retaining the customers you already have. Employing a system like my ROI Matrix enables to you to focus in on building your customer *quantity and quality*. You can market to more leads with better profit margins.

Let your leads lead your bottom line straight up to heavenly revenues. The right tracking system is the only way to make sure you're making the most of them!

ROI Power Plays: Getting a Bead on Your Leads

Look for Suitable Steps for Your Follow-Up Marketing

Every business has their own buying sequence. At any time within that buying sequence, the lead has the opportunity to drop out. That is when you need to follow-through with follow-up marketing.

In this chapter, I detailed those stops for a dental practice; there is a point where a lead calls but does not book an appointment, books an appointment but does not show up, or shows up for the appointment but does not buy the recommended treatment. These are all natural points for a follow-up email or postcard to keep the lead alive and possibly bring him or her around to making a commitment.

Examine your business and see where the natural points are for you to step in and follow up with a lead that threatens to drop out of sight. Develop the right messages, ones that are not too aggressive but are friendly, educational and maybe even offer a special discount and then automate the process of implementing those follow-up "touches."

Automate Your Referral Systems

A personal referral from one of your customers is one of the most powerful ways to generate leads. People tend to listen to friends and family a lot more intently than any sales pitch. Set up an easy online referral system that generates automatic perks or points toward a reward from your business as a customer gives you more and more referrals. Social media is a great place to promote a referral system.

Winnow Your Inactive Leads

As I said, you want to market to your leads until they "buy or die." Now, again, I am not talking about a literal death, but there does comes a time when you may want to consider holding a mass "funeral" for those leads you are still marketing to that are no longer viable.

You or someone on your staff should make the time to go through your list and get rid of those names (after checking out their Database DNA, of course!) that are either extremely unlikely or unable to buy from you in the future. This kind of routine pruning keeps your list lean, mean and effective!

Afterword
Putting ROI Power to Work for YOU!

If you have read this far, you have a pretty good idea of what ROI Power is all about, and hopefully you understand why automated marketing tracking and follow-up systems are so vital in this day and age. The fact is it is an incredibly competitive marketplace out there and you simply cannot afford to "market in the dark" anymore. Blowing your budget on advertising that may actually be *losing* you money is not an option.

That is why I like to say that the automated systems I discussed in the last section of this book are "Simply the Only Way to Know Your Marketing Is Really Working." As a wise man once told me, "Knowing what makes you money is the best way to make MORE money." I have to agree.

Today, we finally have the technology to know, without a doubt, which campaigns and which types of leads bring in the most profits. It is the kind of technology only the big corporations used to be able to afford and they had to do it through expensive, cumbersome and inaccurate methods. Now, it is affordable, instantaneous, easy-to-use, and the information it generates is rock solid.

Here is how it would work if you (or any client) started using my ROI Matrix. When you sign up, you will receive a telephone call in order to set up your account. My staff will automatically insert the dollar amount you give them as the cost for *each* of your advertising or marketing placements that you are tracking into our system.

You will also be provided with a set of unique call tracking numbers. You MUST use these numbers on every form of advertising and marketing that you want to track. These can include:

1. Business cards
2. Invoices
3. Website
4. Yellow pages ads
5. Referral cards
6. Newsletters
7. Billboards
8. Direct mail

9. Letterhead	18. YouTube
10. Email signatures	19. Magazine Ads
11. TV	20. Directories
12. Radio	21. Holiday Cards
13. Brochures	22. T-shirts
14. Promotional items	23. Refrigerator Magnets
15. Google Adwords	24. Appointment Reminder Cards
16. Facebook	
17. Twitter	25. Advertorials

And anything else you want to track!

When those marketing placements generate leads, The ROI Matrix system follows them from first contact through whatever point of the buying process they go through, showing you in real time the "True ROI" of each advertising or marketing placement you decide to track.

For example, when a lead books an appointment at a practice, The ROI Matrix will email your staff the day of that appointment to see if the lead showed up. If they did not show, your staff member clicks "no," and The ROI Matrix automatically connects with your CRM (Infusionsoft®, Constant Contact, etc.) and initiates your "no show" campaign to that particular lead.

If the lead *did* show up, your staff member will automatically be asked follow-up questions such as, "How much was the treatment plan that was recommended?" and "Did the patient accept the plan?" If the answer is "no," then the ROI Matrix again automatically connects with your CRM to initiate your follow-up campaign for patients that do not opt for the recommended care. If the answer is "yes," then the cost of the treatment is recorded and linked to the marketing placement that first brought in the lead.

Again, I am talking about the specifics of the buying sequence at a dental practice. If you have a different kind of business, you will have a different process. The idea is the same.

In any event, throughout this process, the "True ROI" of each marketing placement is constantly recalculated so you can instantly see *which one is generating the most money for your business or practice.* All it takes on the part of you or your staff is a few simple clicks of a mouse.

Without The ROI Matrix, your staff would have to assemble all this data manually. Let's face it, even the best team in the world gets too busy for that kind of constant marketing data. Oversight and human error is bound to occur and that not only can skew your results, but also lose you valuable leads. The ROI Matrix changes all that with an automated system that makes it "brain-dead easy" for your staff to implement. You can add a marketing campaign or placement to your "ROI Matrix" *within minutes* with just *one* phone call to me or my staff!

My particular system also provides, at no extra charge, an incredible array of side benefits to you and your marketing efforts:

- The automatic recording of all incoming calls from generated leads: this enables you to review them with your staff to improve their phone sales performance.

- The automatic transcription of all incoming calls from generated leads: again, to enable staff sales training and also to enable easier follow-up with the leads who called.

- The automatic transfer of captured contact information to your CRM, and to trigger whatever follow-up marketing you want to set up.

- A monthly conference call with your personal ROI Matrix account manager, where you can review your closing statistics and the True ROI for each campaign.

- Notification of every missed lead, through email, text message and phone call

- 24 hour log-in access to your own personal web-based portal, containing all of your information, reports, graphs, charts, and executive summaries with analysis of ALL your tracked marketing campaigns.

- A customized "Whisper" for each number, so your staff knows exactly which marketing message a lead is calling about before they come on the phone.

- A customized voicemail for each number, to give specific information on whatever campaign the lead is calling about, when your staff is not available to answer the phone

- An automatic "scoring" of 1 – 5 for each generated lead call, 1 being the worst (the lead hung up without making an appointment), 5 being the best (the lead made an appointment). This helps you "score" the overall lead quality your marketing is generating.

Those are the basics, and again, I have other Add-ons, such as The Magic Pill for follow-up marketing sequences. To me, systems like The ROI Matrix are really the "Holy Grail" of marketing because they empower you to maximize your ROI in ways never before possible.

With the right technology working 24/7 for your business, you will finally be able to track, to the penny, how much each marketing placement is generating for your business. Imagine knowing without a doubt which marketing and advertising generates the most profits and which leads will be the most loyal and profitable. With that invaluable information, you can put your money strictly towards the marketing and the leads that *make* you money and eliminate wasteful spending on advertising that only drains away your revenues.

Anyway, that is enough preaching from somebody who is not a minister. I do hope this book has taught you a lot of invaluable marketing lessons and I hope you will also consider automating your marketing as described in the last section of the book. If you want a free consultation with me, The ROI Guy, I invite you to email me at Richard@TheROIMatrix.com to set up a time to talk. I will even have a special offer for you if you decide to try out the Matrix.

In the meantime, here is to your ROI Power. I hope it keeps your profits lit up for a long time to come!

www.ingramcontent.com/pod-product-compliance
Lightning Source LLC
Chambersburg PA
CBHW060608200326
41521CB00007B/702